Antique Furniture Reproduction

15 Advanced Projects

John A. Nelson

VNR VAN NOSTRAND REINHOLD COMPANY

To My Wife, Joyce

Printed in the United States of America
Designed by Loudan Enterprises

Published by Van Nostrand Reinhold Company Inc.
135 West 50th Street
New York, New York 10020

Van Nostrand Reinhold Company Limited
Molly Millars Lane
Wokingham, Berkshire RG11 2PY, England

Van Nostrand Reinhold
480 La Trobe Street
Melbourne, Victoria 3000, Australia

Macmillan of Canada
Division of Gage Publishing Limited
164 Commander Boulevard
Agincourt, Ontario M1S 3C7, Canada

16 15 14 13 12 11 10 9 8 7 6 5 4 3 2 1

Library of Congress Cataloging in Publication Data

Nelson, John A., 1935–
   Antique furniture reproduction.

   Includes index.
   1. Furniture making—Amateurs' manuals.   2. Furniture,
Early American.   I. Title.
TT195.N444   1984   749.2914   84-2390
ISBN 0-442-26894-7

Contents

Introduction

No furniture design has been able to capture feelings of warmth and well being as fully and originally as the Early American style does. Because this style is part of our heritage, it holds a lot of nostalgia as well as historical interest. In years past, much of the furniture was made by hand, using (by today's standards) rather primitive tools. Many of these beautiful early pieces were one-of-a-kind items. Today, as it becomes harder and much more expensive to locate and purchase the authentic, original pieces produced by Early American craftsmen, a very satisfying way to acquire your own collection of Early American furniture is to reproduce various pieces yourself.

This text has been written for both the amateur woodworker with limited equipment and the professional with a full woodworking shop. An unusually detailed approach to woodworking is used: each individual part of each project is fully dimensioned and illustrated. This will make the job of both the relatively inexperienced and the advanced woodworker much easier. Because everyone's ability varies and no two craftsmen have the same equipment, very few instructions are given other than simple, general instructions. Once the individual parts are made, the project will fit together as though it came from a simple kit. A final assembly drawing of each project is given to illustrate exactly how the project fits together.

The personal satisfaction felt by earlier craftsmen, accompanied by a certain closeness to history, will be experienced by the woodworker making these projects. All fifteen projects were copied directly from original antiques, so the woodworker will truly be taking a step into the past. Each project is drawn to reproduce the original exactly, even down to the somewhat "odd" construction techniques that were sometimes used. The advanced woodworker may wish to use more modern woodworking techniques, but I suggest that he or she stick to the original, unusual construction methods, regardless of how unconventional they are.

Even today, with the high cost of good wood and accessories, the overall cost of each project is extremely reasonable, and you will get away from the redundant manufactured furniture of today. There is one high-cost factor, and that is time. For those who share a love for our past, our heritage, and Early American furniture, though, it is impossible to put a price on the satisfaction derived from making future heirlooms from historical models.

I sincerely hope that you enjoy making and living with these projects as much as I enjoyed drawing and making them.

General Instructions

Although each project is different, the following general instructions should be followed in every case.

1. Carefully look over *each* individual detail drawing, subassembly drawing, and assembly drawing before beginning any work. Try to visualize how you will make each part.

2. Purchase in advance all materials and hardware needed to complete the project. The materials list accompanying each project is only approximate; the quantities you use will vary depending on how each part is cut. Use the materials list only as a guide or estimation. Try to visualize what you will need, and be ready to substitute lumber sizes—lumber yards rarely have exactly the size and type of material specified for every item on your list. Do not be afraid to use wood that has splits or water stains—these help to produce a very old look and add character to your project.

3. Make sure that you own or have access to all the tools needed to complete the project.

4. It is *extremely* important that all cuts be make at *exactly* 90° (unless the instructions explicitly direct otherwise), so take extra care to measure and make all cuts accurately.

5. Make each individual part according to the corresponding detail drawing. More than one part of the same design is sometimes needed. Be sure that all such parts are exactly the same size and shape. Sometimes parts are made in exact opposite pairs, or mirror images. This will be noted on the detail drawing by the notes:

1 REQ'D AS SHOWN
1 REQ'D OPPOSITE SHOWN

It is important that such pairs be mirror images of each other, with exactly the same size and shape in all other respects.

6. Before starting to put together any subassembly or assembly, sand all constituent parts smooth.

7. Before gluing any subassembly or assembly, "dry-fit" the *complete* unit to check that all parts fit together *exactly.*

8. Carefully glue the parts together, and clamp them if possible. Wipe all excess glue away with a slightly damp rag before the glue hardens. *All exposed glue must be removed before staining;* it will otherwise appear white on the surface.

9. As you assemble each project, be sure each part is flush—that is, tight-fitting—and "square." Do not rush this step: check and recheck before the glue dries or sets. Try to use clamps wherever possible.

10. After the glue dries or sets, resand the completed project.

11. As these projects are copies of old antiques, they will not look authentic if they have a shiny brand-new appearance. In most cases, they will look much more like real antiques if they are distressed slightly. There are many ways to do this—from hitting the final project with a chain to shooting it with a shotgun. Some fanatics on the "state of the art" even bury their projects in the ground for six months. This is a little extreme. Experiment to see what works the best for you. I have a pea stone walkway

and have found that simply rolling the final project in the pea stones adds a nice distressed look.

12. It is a good idea to clean your workshop completely and to allow time for the dust to settle before starting the finishing processes.

13. Completely wipe the project with a cloth that is slightly dampened with turpentine. All surfaces must be dust-free and thoroughly dry before the stain is applied. The finishing process, if done correctly, will take as long as the making of the project. Don't rush this step: it is what really stands out and gives the project a professional look.

14. There are many kinds of finishes available today. If I apply stain at all, I like a very light stain with two coats of hand-rubbed tung oil. Tung oil lets the wood "breathe," which in turn allows it to age nicely over time. If you use tung oil, do not wax the project afterward: just apply a light coat of good-grade lemon oil.

15. I like to use a wash coat on my projects to give them a very old look. A wash coat is simply a mixture of ¼ part dull black paint and ¾ part thinner. Mix the components and put the mixture in an airtight jar for storage. Simply wipe the wash coat over the entire project and wipe it right off. If you have distressed the project, the black of the wash coat will accent the effect, adhering to the cracks, joints, and corners of the project and adding 100 years to its appearance. Allow this to dry thoroughly, and then add a light top coat of tung oil over the wash coat.

16. Because these are antique projects, try to locate old square-cut nails and use them. If old square-cut nails are not available locally, you can get them from the Tremont Nail Company in Wareham, Massachusetts, which still makes them exactly as they were made 100 years ago. Write for the company's catalog; its address is listed under suppliers at the end of this book. I think you will enjoy using old-style nails, and they add so very much to your project.

Final note: Every attempt has been made to verify each dimension and the accuracy of all information. As you proceed, remember to recheck each dimension and dry-fit each mating part. Some parts will have to be custom-fitted to ensure a perfect fit.

Woodworking Safety

Whatever your level of skill and expertise, you would do well to review the following list of suggestions for woodworking safety.

1. Do not allow children and pets in the workshop area.
2. Keep all power equipment locked and (if possible) stored out of children's reach when not in use.
3. Store your tools in a well-organized manner; do not leave them hanging over table edges or lying on the floor.
4. Keep floors in the workshop area clean; sawdust can be very slippery.
5. Never leave protruding nails in boards.
6. Do not wear loose clothing or jewelry that could become entangled in moving parts of machinery. Remove rings before operating equipment. Hair long enough to fall forward onto machinery must be secured out of harm's way.
7. Be sure that wood chisels, files, awls, hammers, and mallets have sturdy handles that hold their tools firmly.
8. Keep all tools in good repair. Do not allow cutting edges to become dull.
9. Use the correct tool for the job—for example, never use a chisel to drive screws—and read and follow the manufacturer's recommended procedures for operating any tool or piece of equipment.
10. Always wear safety glasses, even when working with hand tools. The glasses provide protection against flying woodchips, sawdust, and metal projectiles such as broken nail heads and improperly struck nails.
11. Turn power tools off before adjusting the position of the stock or tool.
12. Keep fingers and hands away from the cutting edge of tools. If you are using a table saw, make push sticks out of a couple of pieces of solid scrap wood and use these to guide the wood you are cutting past the blade.
13. Make sure the piece you are working on is steady on its base or supports; this will minimize the likelihood of its tipping or bucking while you are working on it.
14. When working with a wood chisel or other sharp tool, use a vise or clamp (not your hand) to hold the wood.
15. Wood chisel, knife, and plane strokes should be directed away from your body; push away from your body with each stroke.
16. Do not talk to or interrupt anyone who is working on a machine, and do not turn your attention from the machine while you are working at it. Keep your eyes focused on the cutting action at all times.
17. Do not leave any power tool plugged in or running unattended.
18. Do not carry more tools than you can handle safely.
19. Never run in the workshop.
20. Use good common sense, and always consider the safety of others.

Long Bench

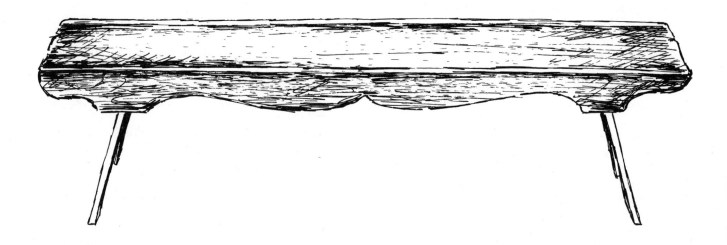

This bench is a copy of a unique piece made of maple. The original was painted blue at one time, but the paint was later removed. This is a very simple project, and the bench is so sturdy that it can be used for many purposes. Not much is known about the past uses the original was put to, but the copy could be lengthened or shortened slightly to fit almost anywhere. It would make an excellent bench for your favorite plants.

MATERIALS

(Recommended wood: butternut or maple)
one 1-by-12-inch 8-foot-long board
one 1-by-10-inch 4-foot-long board
Square-cut nails
Sandpaper—medium and fine
Water putty
Wood glue
Stain or paint of your choice
Tung oil
Wash

INSTRUCTIONS

Lay out and cut out the side trim, feet, and end braces (figures 1, 3, and 4). Sand all surfaces, sanding the parts in pairs so that each pair matches. Cut out the main board and center brace (figures 2 and 5) to size, and sand them all over. If hardwood is used, drill slightly undersize pilot holes for the square-cut nails. Assemble as shown in the assembly drawings.

FINISH

Distress and resand; then paint or stain to suit. Add a wash coat to make the bench look older.

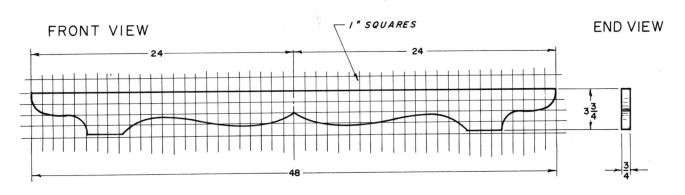

① SIDE TRIM
2 REQ'D

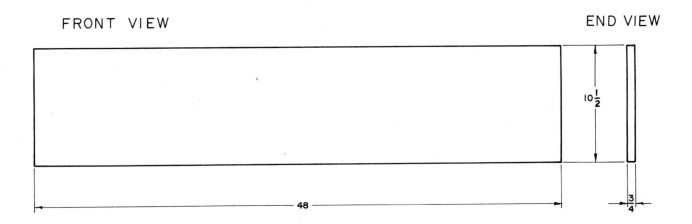

② MAIN BOARD
1 REQ'D

SIDE VIEW   FRONT VIEW

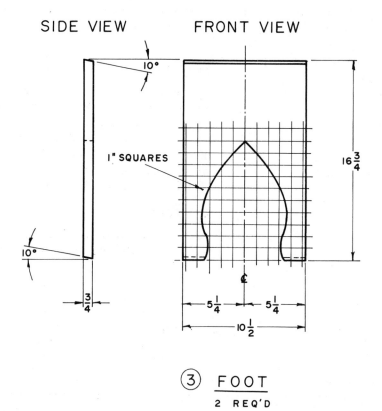

1" SQUARES

$16\frac{3}{4}$

$5\frac{1}{4}$ $5\frac{1}{4}$

$10\frac{1}{2}$

$\frac{3}{4}$

10°

10°

③ FOOT
2 REQ'D

FRONT VIEW   END VIEW

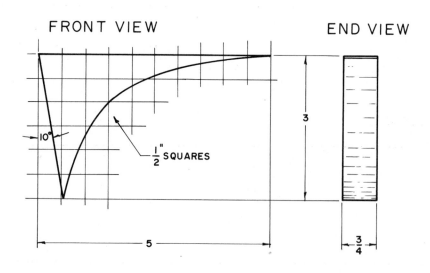

10°

$\frac{1}{2}$" SQUARES

3

5

$\frac{3}{4}$

④ END BRACE
2 REQ'D

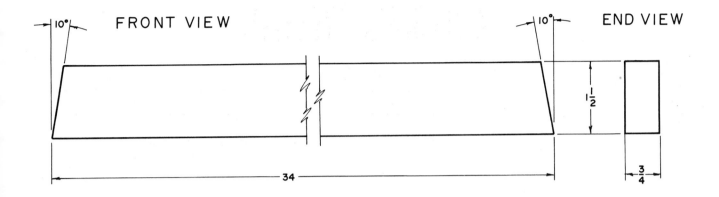

FRONT VIEW END VIEW

10° 10°

$1\frac{1}{2}$

34

$\frac{3}{4}$

⑤ CENTER BRACE
1 REQ'D

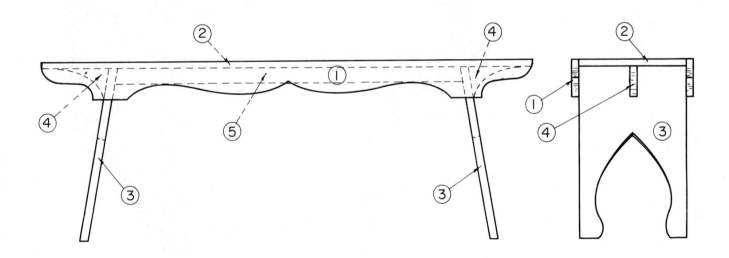

② ④ ②

① ① ①

④ ④

⑤ ④

③ ③ ③

⑥ ASSEMBLY

Child's Trunk

Small children wanted to be like their parents and therefore needed a trunk of their own to hold their favorite possessions. The original of this particular trunk was made of a very poor grade of pine and was assembled exactly as shown, except that it had a cowhide covering, held in place by brass tacks. The inside of these trunks was wallpapered, usually with paper bearing a small pattern. Look for old hardware to use for the handles and lock. Much of today's hardware does not capture the antique flare. These trunks usually had a lot of rough treatment, so do not be afraid to distress your new "old" trunk thoroughly. If the antiquing is done correctly, the trunk will appear to be 150 years old.

MATERIALS
(Recommended wood: pine)
one 1-by-12-inch 2-foot-long board
one ½-by-10-inch 6-foot-long board
one ¼-by-12-inch 2-foot-long board
two antique-style handles
one lock with key
sixteen sixpenny finish nails
Square-cut nails
Brass tacks
Sandpaper—medium and fine
Water putty
Wood glue
Stain of your choice
Tung oil
Dull black paint
Wash

INSTRUCTIONS
Lay out and cut out the bottom, front, rear, end, and top boards (figures 1, 2, 3, and 4) to size per the detail drawings. Sand only the inside surfaces at this time. Assemble the parts as shown in figure 5, using only glue and finish nails. Set all the finish nails and, using wood putty, fill all nail holes and joints. Roughly trim the overhang of the top board (figure 4) with a plane, and completely sand the sides, top, and bottom. Carefully scribe a line 5⅞ inches up from the bottom, and then cut along it, all around. *Important:* do not cut until all sides are sanded absolutely smooth. Add the bottom supports (figure 6) to the bottom, 1 inch in from the sides. Distress the trunk, and resand. Make original-style "tin" hinges as shown in the four-step hinge assembly (figure 7). Cut pieces from any large tin can available (step 1); bend these in half (step 2); and paint them with dull black paint and assemble with ¹⁄₁₆-inch-diameter wire, approximately 2⅜ inches long (steps 3 and 4).

FINISH
Distress, resand, and add stain and tung oil. Cut 12 square-cut nails, so that each is ½ inch long, and assemble the top half of the trunk with the bottom half, using the 12 cut nails—6 for each hinge. Add handles at the ends, using the same size square-cut nails. Add a lock to suit; if possible, nail it in place. The original did not have screws anywhere in its assembly. Add brass tacks along the edges, with approximately ¾-inch spacing between each. Sometimes small trunks had designs or initials on the top. Be careful to plan all work ahead of time, and don't get too carried away. The original small trunk was covered in leather and actually bore two sets of initials— the second set being a later addition. Things like this make an antique even more interesting.

FRONT VIEW

END VIEW

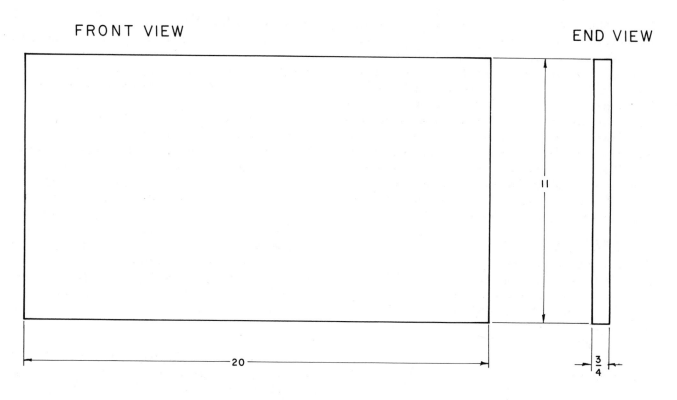

① BOTTOM BOARD
I REQ'D

FRONT VIEW

END VIEW

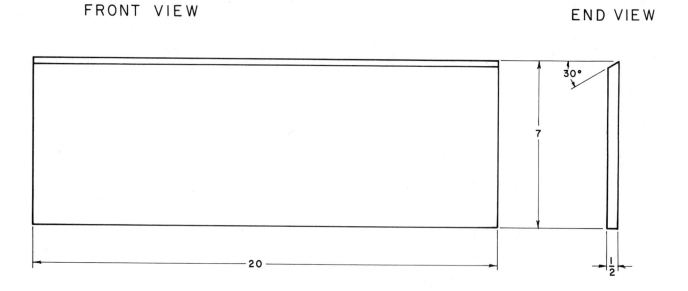

② FRONT / REAR BOARD
2 REQ'D

FRONT VIEW   SIDE VIEW

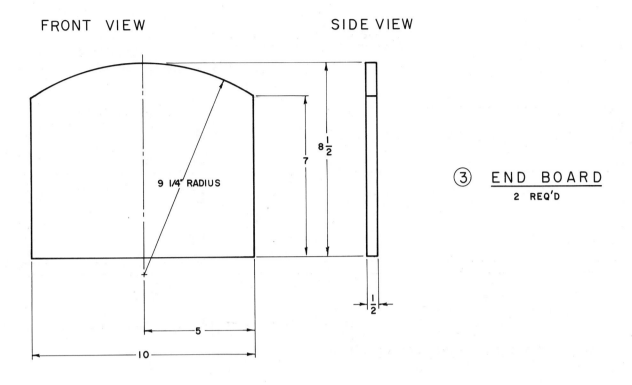

③ END BOARD
2 REQ'D

FRONT VIEW   END VIEW

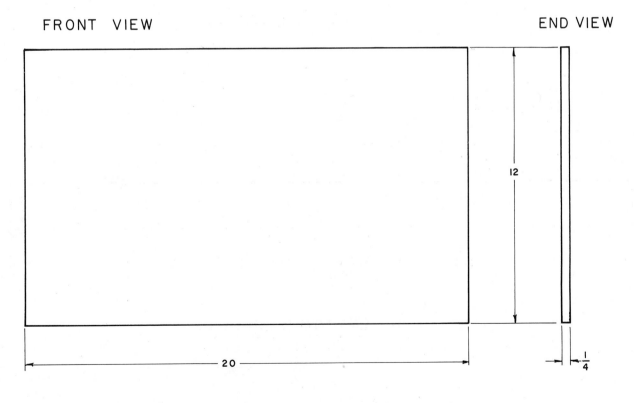

④ TOP BOARD
1 REQ'D

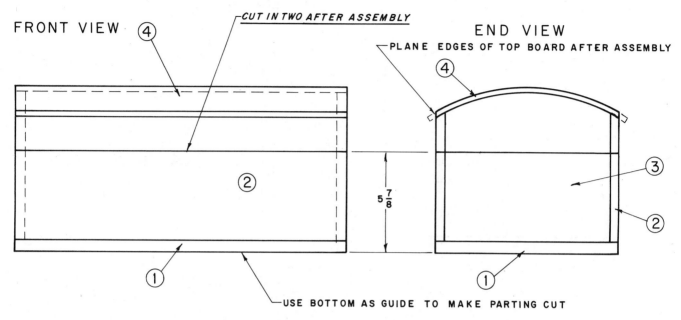

FRONT VIEW   ④

CUT IN TWO AFTER ASSEMBLY

END VIEW

PLANE EDGES OF TOP BOARD AFTER ASSEMBLY

④

②

③

②

$5\frac{7}{8}$

①

①

USE BOTTOM AS GUIDE TO MAKE PARTING CUT

SAND ALL SURFACES BEFORE CUTTING IN TWO

⑤   SUBASSEMBLY
1 REQ'D

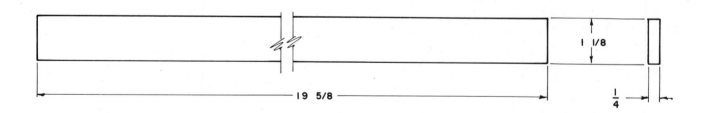

TOP VIEW

END VIEW

1 1/8

19 5/8

$\frac{1}{4}$

⑥   BOTTOM SUPPORT
2 REQ'D

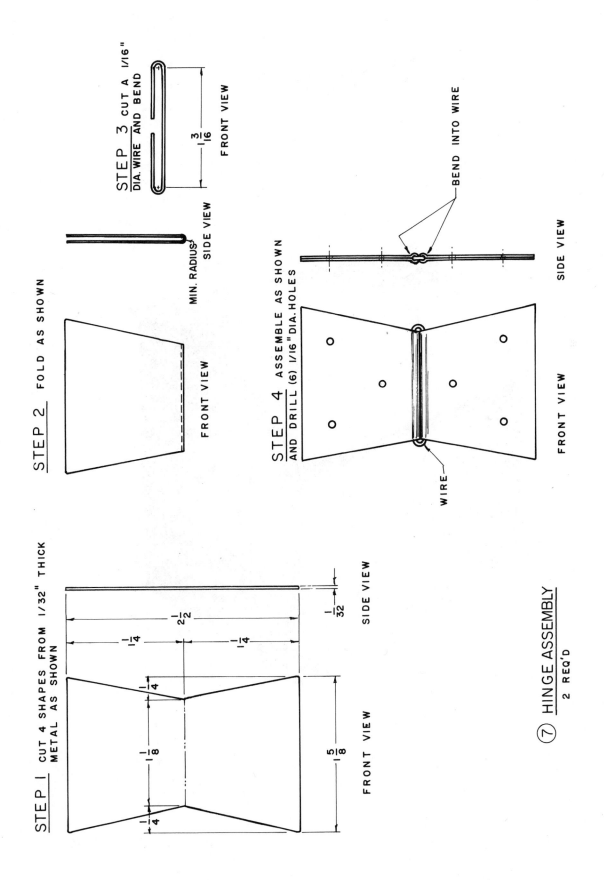

Woodbox

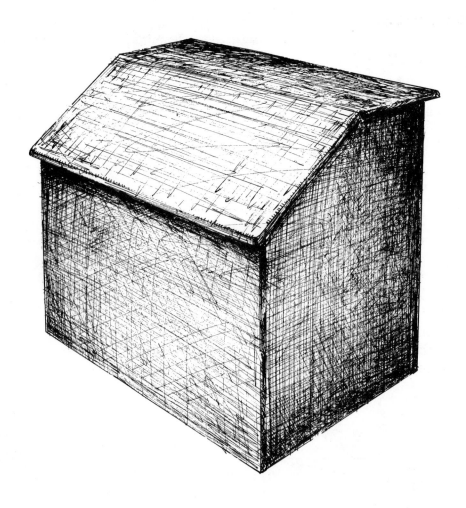

The woodbox is one of the simplest projects in this book. Given the current popularity of the woodstove, it will be a very functional project. Woodboxes came in many sizes and shapes.Some had covers; others, no cover. Some had dividers to separate the kindling from the "all nighters." Most were made of pine or poplar, and most were painted. A woodbox makes an excellent project to stencil because you can take all kinds of liberties and create a true one-of-a-kind item. A knob or hanger for stove shovels, tongs, or brooms may be added to give the woodbox a really functional look. As drawn, a piano hinge is used to attach the lid to the box. The original woodbox had two leather hinges, and these were followed by two (now very old and worn) strap hinges, nailed in place.

MATERIALS

(Recommended wood: pine)
four 1-by-12-inch 12-foot-long boards
one 1-by-4-inch 12-foot-long board
one 36-inch-long piano hinge (cut to size)
thirty-six square-cut nails (old, if possible)
Sandpaper—medium and fine
Water putty
Wood glue
Stain or paint of your choice
Tung oil
Wash

INSTRUCTIONS

Glue up the side and bottom panels and the lid (figures 1, 2, 3, 4, and 6), so that they are slightly oversize. For example, the end panels (figure 1) should be glued up to approximately 23 by 36 inches. Cut them to exact size and shape after the glue sets. Cut to size the remaining parts (figures 5, 7, 8, and 9), and assemble them as shown in figure 10. Take care to keep all sides square. Use square-cut nails spaced approximately 3 to 4 inches apart. Do not set the nails; let them show (as the original ones did). If old, rusty, square-cut nails can be found, use them—it will really add an authentic look. Sand all over and paint the inside with a wash coat of one part dull black paint and three parts thinner. Distress, round the front inside surface edge to add a worn look, and resand.

FINISH

The woodbox's finish can be either a stain or an antique color. To add special character to this woodbox, paint it and then add an antique stencil to suit. After painting or staining, add a light coat of tung oil and apply the wash coat.

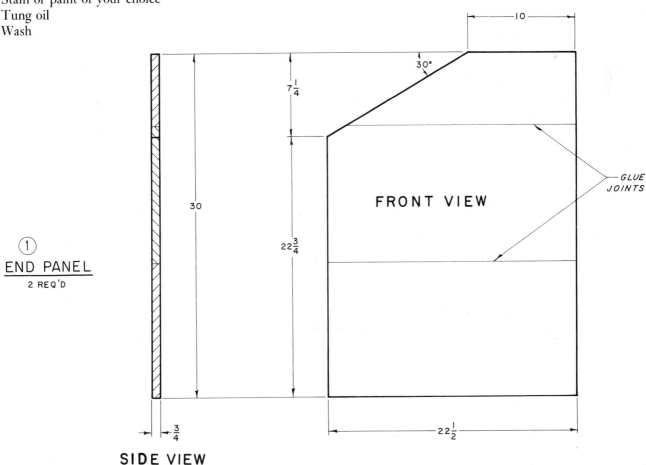

① END PANEL
2 REQ'D

SIDE VIEW

FRONT VIEW

GLUE JOINTS

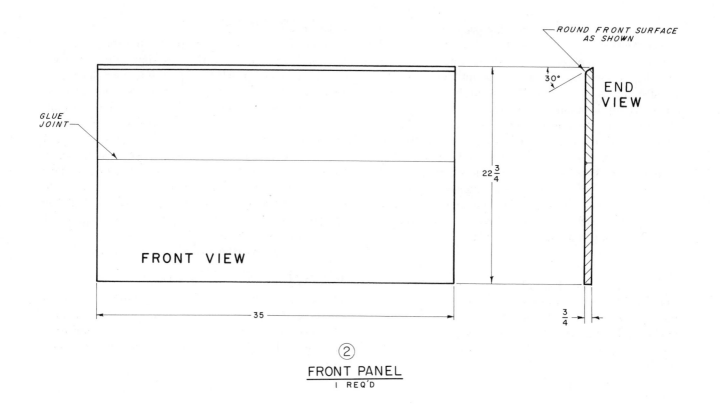

ROUND FRONT SURFACE
AS SHOWN

GLUE
JOINT

30°

END
VIEW

22 3/4

FRONT VIEW

35

3/4

② FRONT PANEL
I REQ'D

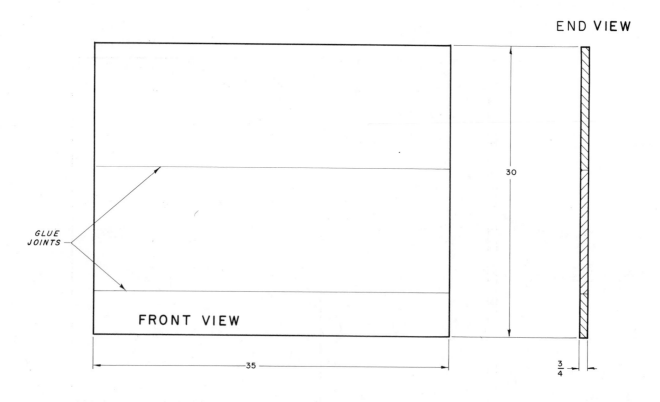

END VIEW

GLUE
JOINTS

30

FRONT VIEW

35

3/4

③ REAR PANEL
I REQ'D

END VIEW

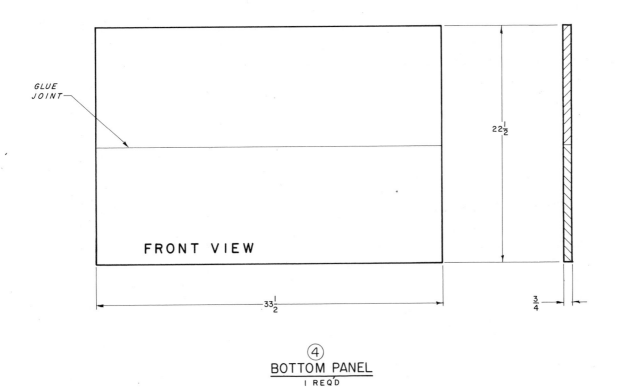

GLUE
JOINT

FRONT VIEW

$22\frac{1}{2}$

$33\frac{1}{2}$

$\frac{3}{4}$

④
BOTTOM PANEL
I REQ'D

END VIEW

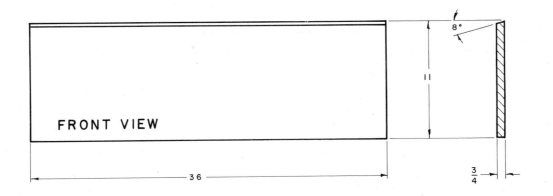

FRONT VIEW

8°

11

3 6

$\frac{3}{4}$

⑤
TOP PANEL
I REQ'D

GLUE JOINT

END VIEW

FRONT VIEW

15½

36

22°

30°

ROUND EDGES

¾

⑥
<u>LID</u>
I REQ'D

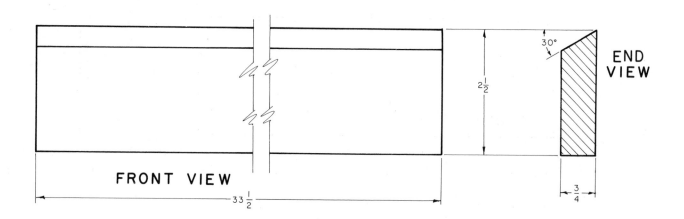

FRONT VIEW

END
VIEW

30°

2½

33½

¾

⑦
<u>FRONT BRACE</u>
I REQ'D

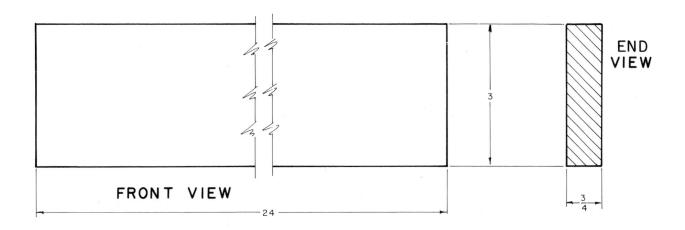

END VIEW

FRONT VIEW

3

24

3/4

⑧ BOTTOM SUPPORT
2 REQ'D

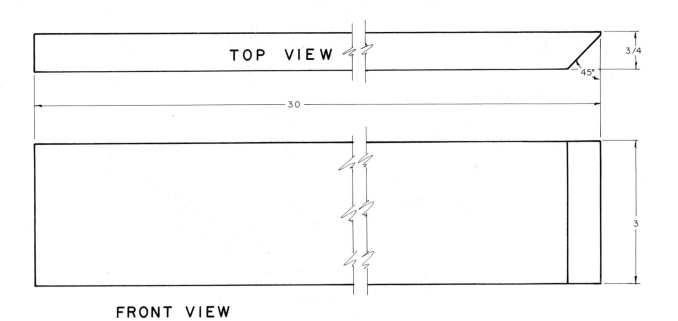

TOP VIEW

3/4

45°

30

3

FRONT VIEW

⑨ REAR SUPPORT
2 REQ'D

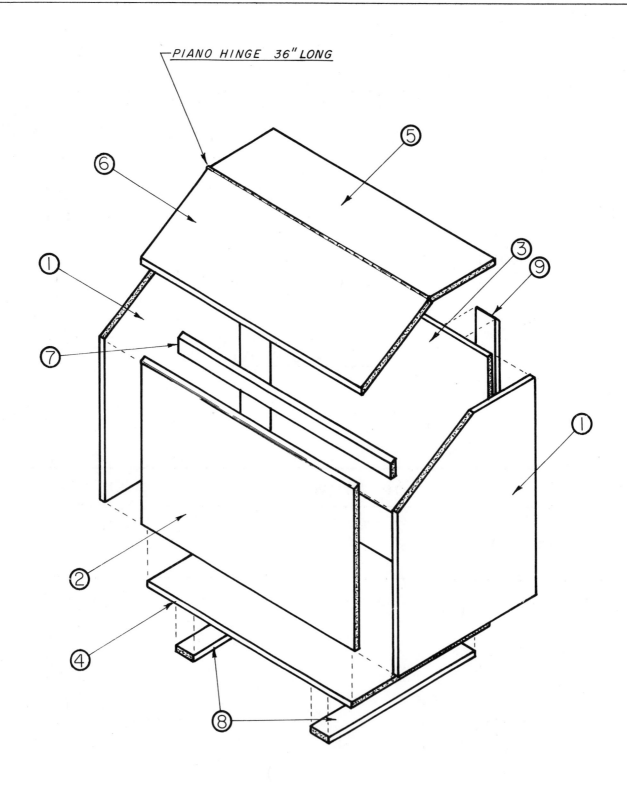

PIANO HINGE 36" LONG

⑩ **WOODBOX ASSEMBLY**

Silver Tray

This authentic silverware tray is in a style popular around 1800. A visit to any flea market will uncover two or three of these trays, selling for thirty to forty dollars each. Why they faded from popularity is a mystery to me—they are very handy to have and use. The parts of this project are fairly easy to make, but, unless you have five hands, the project is a little difficult to assemble. The center divider board should be cut to fit after the main assembly has been put together. The original silverware tray was made of pine, but a more elegant tray could be constructed out of cherry or walnut. In order to complete this project, a planer is needed to produce the ⅜- and ¼-inch-thick material from the ½-inch-thick board.

MATERIALS

(Recommended wood: cherry or walnut)
one ½-by-8-inch 4-foot-long board
one ⁵⁄₄-by-⁵⁄₄-inch 8-inch-long board (or 1-inch-diameter dowel)
eighteen small square-cut nails
Water putty
Wood glue
Sandpaper—medium and fine
Stain of your choice
Tung oil
Wash

INSTRUCTIONS

Lay out ½-inch squares on a piece of 8-by-13-inch cardboard. Cut out and trace this shape on the wood. It is a good idea to locate the centers of the two ¹⁵⁄₁₆-inch holes and drill them before cutting the rest of the pattern. Cut the overall length oversize, and trim it to fit later. Lay out and cut to size the side boards, end boards and bottom (figures 2, 3, and 4). Take care to cut all angles as noted. It is important to get these as close as possible to ensure a good, tight fit between mating parts. Either with a lathe or by hand, make the handle (figure 5). No two handles were ever exactly the same, so even a hand-carved one will look authentic. Dry-fit all parts before final assembly; trim if necessary. Four and one-half hands are needed to assemble the four sides, so it is a good idea to get help for this part of the project. Drill small pilot holes before nailing through the hardwood, as the nails are to go very close to the ends of the material.

FINISH

If all the parts were dry-fitted before assembly, all the joints should be tight! If they are not, add water putty as needed, and then sand all over. Round the edges slightly, distress, and resand.

Apply stain and tung oil to suit. Tung oil is especially good to use because it is nontoxic and gives an authentic look to the project. Add a wash coat and wipe dry. Add another light coat of tung oil.

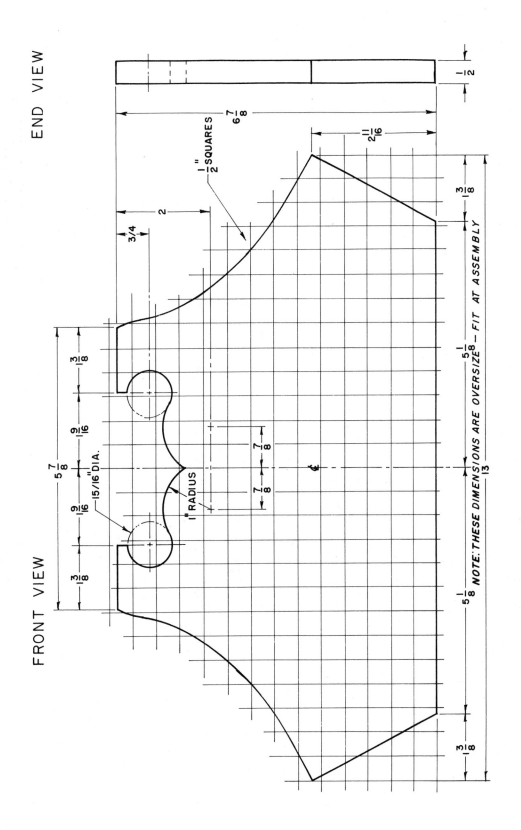

END VIEW

FRONT VIEW

1 CENTER DIVIDER
I REQ'D

NOTE: THESE DIMENSIONS ARE OVERSIZE — FIT AT ASSEMBLY

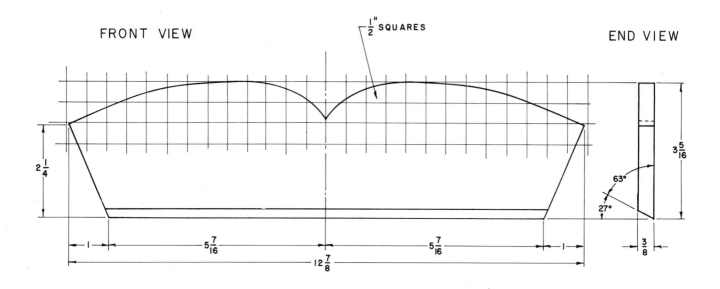

FRONT VIEW

½" SQUARES

END VIEW

2¼

3 5/16

63°

27°

3/8

1

5 7/16

5 7/16

1

12 7/8

② <u>SIDE BOARD</u>
2 REQ'D

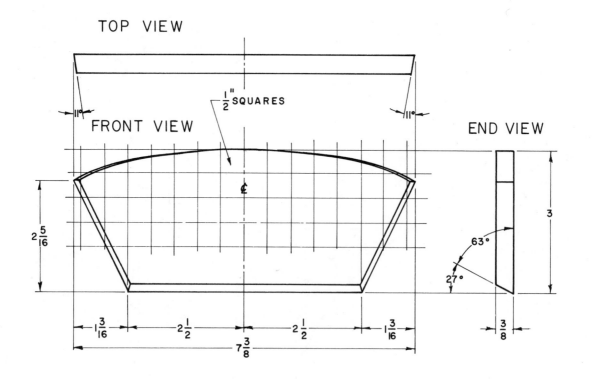

TOP VIEW

½" SQUARES

11°

FRONT VIEW

11°

END VIEW

¢

2 5/16

3

63°

27°

3/8

1 3/16

2½

2½

1 3/16

7 3/8

③ <u>END BOARD</u>
2 REQ'D

TOP VIEW

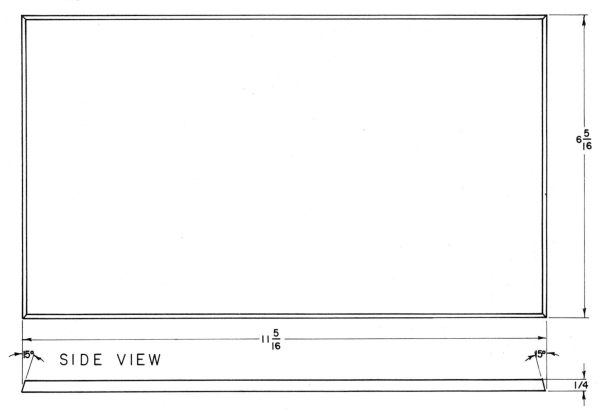

$6\frac{5}{16}$

$11\frac{5}{16}$

SIDE VIEW

15°

15°

1/4

④ BOTTOM
I REQ'D

SIDE VIEW

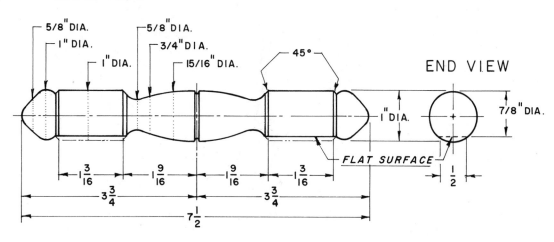

5/8" DIA.

5/8" DIA.

1" DIA.

3/4" DIA.

1" DIA.

15/16" DIA.

45°

END VIEW

1" DIA.

7/8" DIA.

FLAT SURFACE

$\frac{1}{2}$

$1\frac{3}{16}$

$1\frac{9}{16}$

$1\frac{9}{16}$

$1\frac{3}{16}$

$3\frac{3}{4}$

$3\frac{3}{4}$

$7\frac{1}{2}$

⑤ HANDLE
I REQ'D

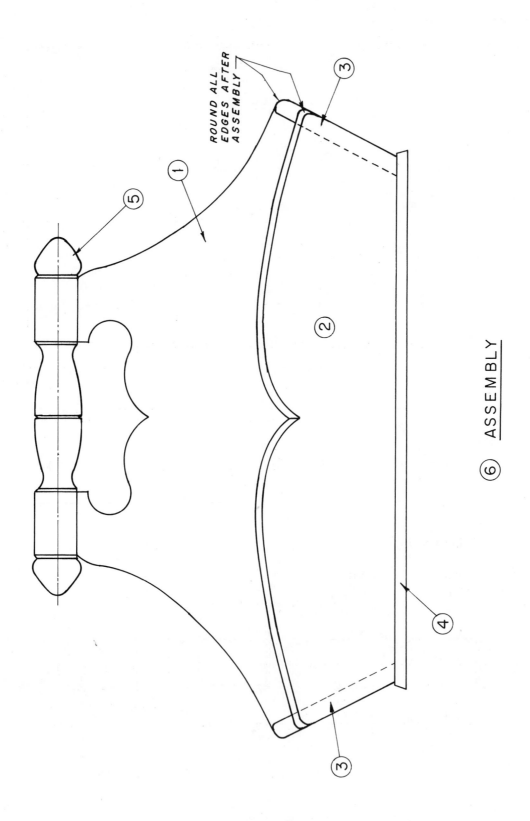

ROUND ALL
EDGES AFTER
ASSEMBLY

ASSEMBLY

Slipper-Foot Table

The most interesting feature of this little table is its slipper-foot legs. They give it elegance and turn it into a more formal piece of furniture. This project should be popular with both inexperienced and advanced woodworkers. The only tricky part is the cutting of the dovetails on the legs and of the corresponding sockets on the center column. This particular table is unusual in that most tables of this style and period had round or oval tops. The rectangular top makes it special as well as easier.

MATERIALS

(Recommended wood: cherry or butternut)
one 3-by-3-inch 2-foot-long board
one 1-by-6-inch 5-foot-long board
one 1-by-10-inch 3-foot-long board
two #10 flat head wood screws—1 inch long each
Water putty
Wood glue
Sandpaper—medium and fine
Tung oil
Wash
#0000 steel wool

INSTRUCTIONS

Turn the main post (figure 1) to shape, per the detail drawing. (Do not cut notches at the bottom end yet).

Carefully lay out and cut out a cardboard pattern of the legs. Retrace the pattern on the piece of 1-by-6-inch wood after adjusting it so as to get the correct direction of the grain and to capture the most interesting grain pattern. Number each leg (1, 2, and 3) at its tail, in order to custom fit each to the main post. Carefully lay out three even spaces, 120° apart, at the bottom of the main post. Using the tail of each leg as a pattern, scribe the tail shape at the end. Cut these notches by hand and chisel out each notch. Check each leg for tight fit as you proceed.

Be sure to number each of the grooves to correspond to the legs. Cut the notches slightly undersize in order to have a tight fit. Glue together the top board (figure 3) and cut to size. Setting your saw at 30°, cut a 60° taper on all edges, as shown in figure 3. Cut to size the support (figure 4), center it, and screw it to the bottom of the top board. Assemble as shown in the assembly drawing.

FINISH

Sand all over and apply tung oil. (A light coat of stain may be applied but the piece will look better over time if the wood is allowed to age by itself). Apply two or three coats of tung oil, allowing each to dry thoroughly and sanding the table between coats with #0000 steel wool.

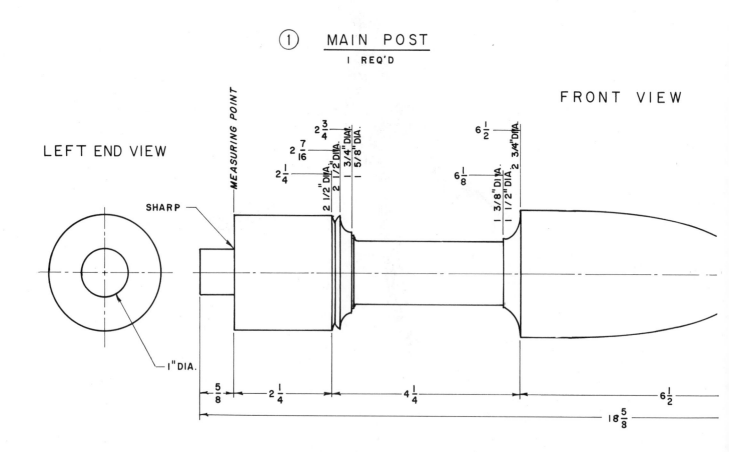

① MAIN POST
I REQ'D

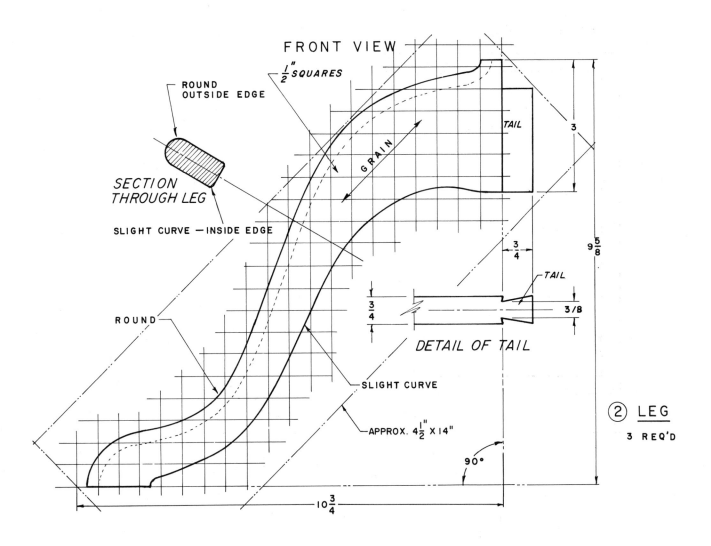

FRONT VIEW

½" SQUARES

ROUND OUTSIDE EDGE

SECTION THROUGH LEG

SLIGHT CURVE — INSIDE EDGE

GRAIN

TAIL

3

9⅝

¾

TAIL

¾

3/8

DETAIL OF TAIL

ROUND

SLIGHT CURVE

APPROX. 4½" X 14"

② LEG

3 REQ'D

90°

10¾

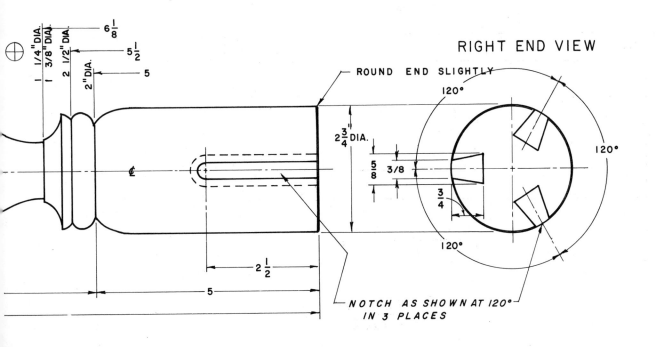

6⅛

5½

5

1 1/4" DIA.

1 3/8" DIA.

2 1/2" DIA.

2" DIA.

₡

ROUND END SLIGHTLY

RIGHT END VIEW

120°

120°

120°

120°

2¾" DIA.

5/8

3/8

¾

2½

5

NOTCH AS SHOWN AT 120° IN 3 PLACES

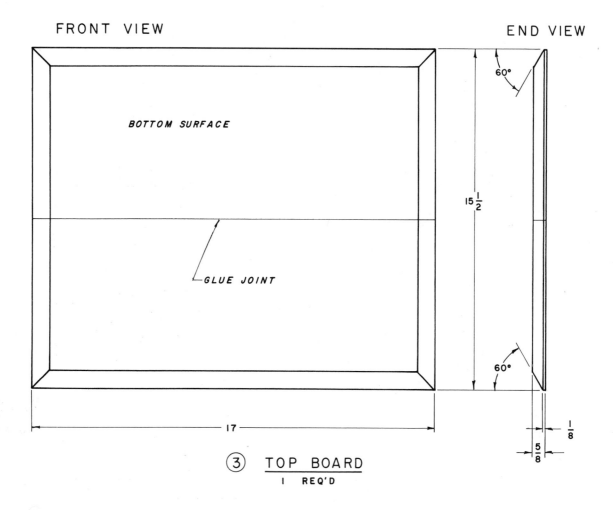

FRONT VIEW   END VIEW

BOTTOM SURFACE

60°

60°

15 1/2

GLUE JOINT

17

1/8

5/8

③ TOP BOARD
        I REQ'D

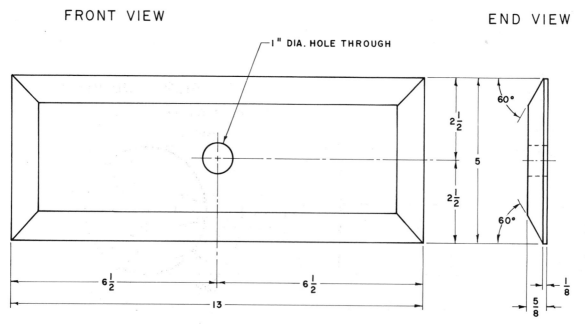

FRONT VIEW   END VIEW

I" DIA. HOLE THROUGH

60°

2 1/2

5

2 1/2

60°

6 1/2   6 1/2

13

1/8

5/8

④ SUPPORT
        I REQ'D

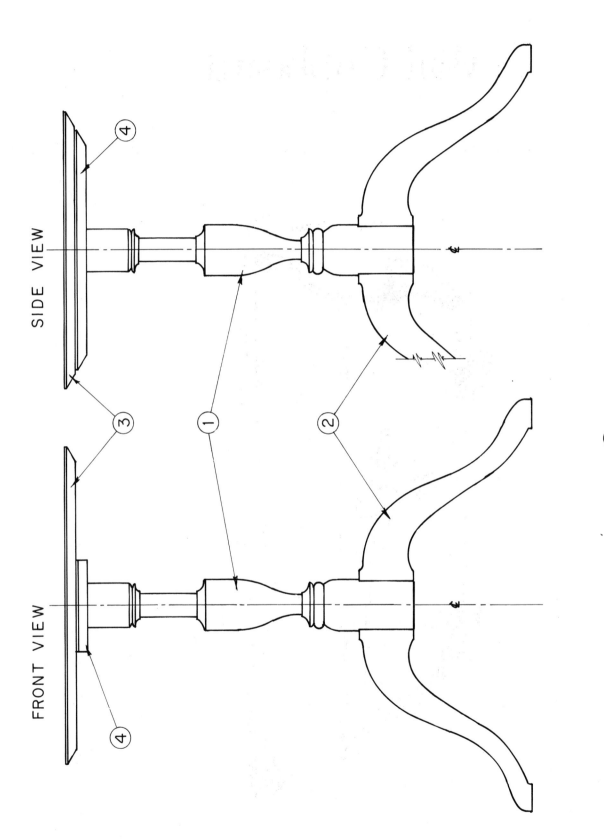

SIDE VIEW

FRONT VIEW

⑤ <u>ASSEMBLY</u>

Wall Cupboard

This unique wall cupboard was found in an antique shop in southern New Hampshire. It was so different and unusual that I just had to have one. All hinges and latches are made of wood and actually work very nicely. The original is made of pine and painted, although the design would also look nice in cherry, unpainted. It would make an excellent bathroom cupboard for those extras that never quite fit into the medicine cabinet. This project will not take very long to construct and will add a lot to any room in which it is hung.

MATERIALS

(Recommended wood: pine or cherry)
two ½-by-10-inch 6-foot long boards
one ⅜-inch-diameter dowel—3 feet long
one #10 flat head wood screw (brass, if possible)
thirty-six square-cut nails
Water putty
Wood glue
Sandpaper—medium and fine
Paint—antique color
Tung oil
Wash

INSTRUCTIONS

Glue up material for the back board and front panel (figures 1 and 3), if necessary. Cut these to size as shown in the detail drawings. Notch the sides (figure 2) and cut to shape. Cut and sand the shelves to size as shown in figure 4. Cut the door from the side panels as shown in figure 3-B and set it aside. Assemble all of the above parts as illustrated in figure 5. Use the door (figure 3-B) as a spacer when assembling the two front panel sides (figures 3-A and 3-C). Leave approximately 1/16-inch spaces between the three parts of the front panels.

Carefully cut out the hinge strap, hinge support, latch guide, and latch stop (figures 6, 7, 9, and 10). Sand all surfaces. Glue up the material for the latch (figure 8) as shown in the detail drawings. Add the door trim—the parts shown in figures 6, 8, and 9, plus the brass wood screws—as shown in figure 11. Be sure to predrill pilot holes before nailing the small wooden parts, to ensure that they will not split. Place the door subassembly in position with a small space at each side. Temporarily tack the door in place with very thin finish nails, leaving the heads extended about ⅛ inch, so they can be easily removed. Glue and nail the hinge support and latch stop (figures 7 and 10) in place, with the door temporarily tacked in place. Don't forget to predrill the pilot holes before nailing. After the glue dries, remove the tacks from the door and check its operation. It should open and close very smoothly. If it turns tightly, sand the dowel pins slightly so that the door opens and closes easily without any bind.

FINISH

Sand all over, distress, and resand. Apply a light coat of tung oil, and when that has dried apply paint of your choice. Sand the edges of the door to add a "worn" look and apply a coat of wash. Wipe clean and apply a final coat of tung oil.

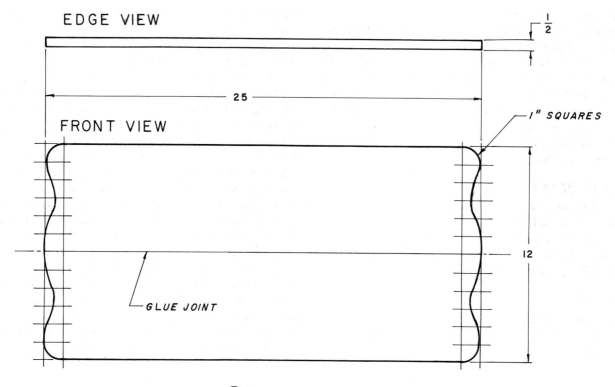

EDGE VIEW

$\frac{1}{2}$

25

FRONT VIEW

1" SQUARES

12

GLUE JOINT

① BACK BOARD
1 REQ'D

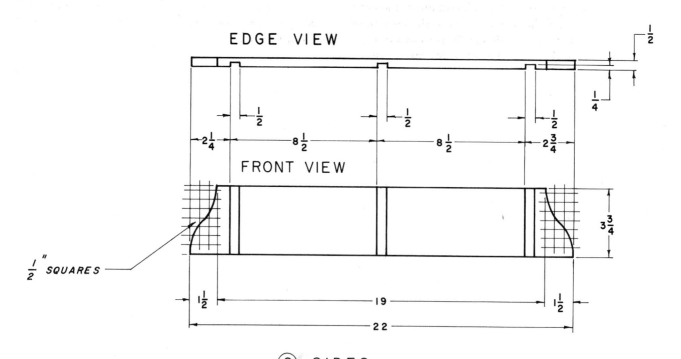

EDGE VIEW

$\frac{1}{2}$

$\frac{1}{2}$ $\frac{1}{2}$ $\frac{1}{2}$

$\frac{1}{4}$

$2\frac{1}{4}$ $8\frac{1}{2}$ $8\frac{1}{2}$ $2\frac{3}{4}$

FRONT VIEW

$3\frac{3}{4}$

$\frac{1}{2}$" SQUARES

$1\frac{1}{2}$ 19 $1\frac{1}{2}$

22

② SIDES
1 REQ'D AS SHOWN
1 REQ'D OPPOSITE SHOWN

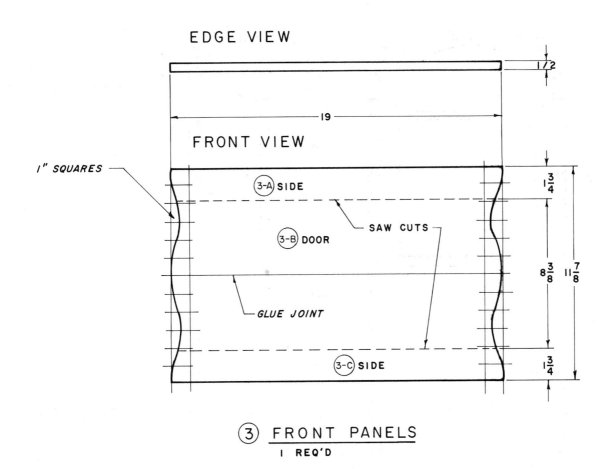

EDGE VIEW

FRONT VIEW

1" SQUARES

3-A SIDE

SAW CUTS

3-B DOOR

GLUE JOINT

3-C SIDE

③ FRONT PANELS
1 REQ'D

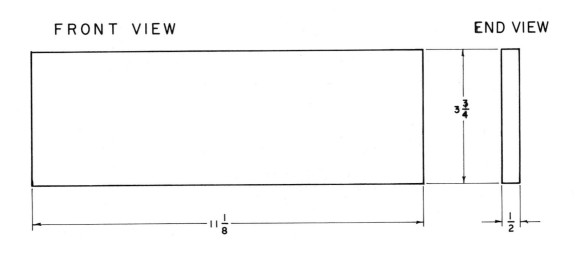

FRONT VIEW

END VIEW

④ SHELF
3 REQ'D

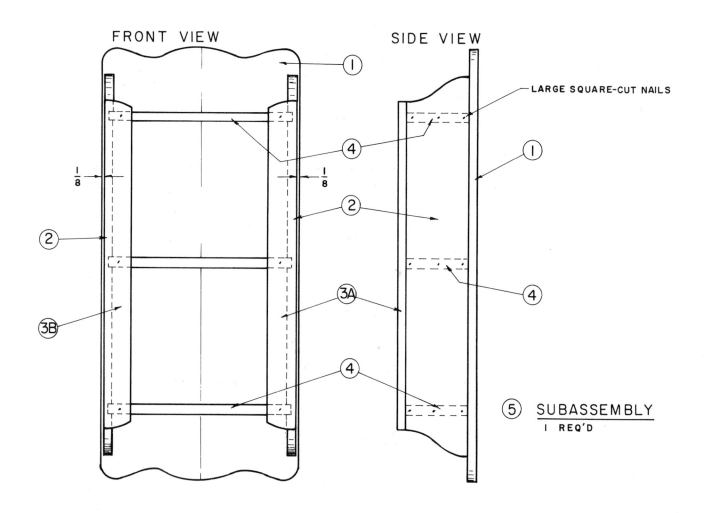

FRONT VIEW   SIDE VIEW

LARGE SQUARE-CUT NAILS

(5) <u>SUBASSEMBLY</u>
I REQ'D

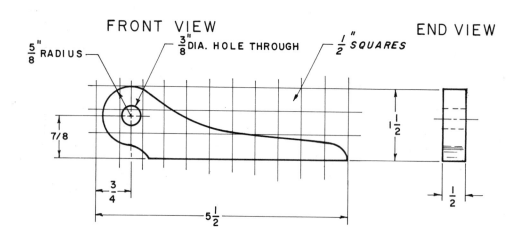

FRONT VIEW   END VIEW

$\frac{5}{8}$" RADIUS $\frac{3}{8}$" DIA. HOLE THROUGH $\frac{1}{2}$" SQUARES

$\frac{7}{8}$ $1\frac{1}{2}$

$\frac{3}{4}$ $\frac{1}{2}$

$5\frac{1}{2}$

(6) <u>HINGE STRAP</u>
2 REQ'D

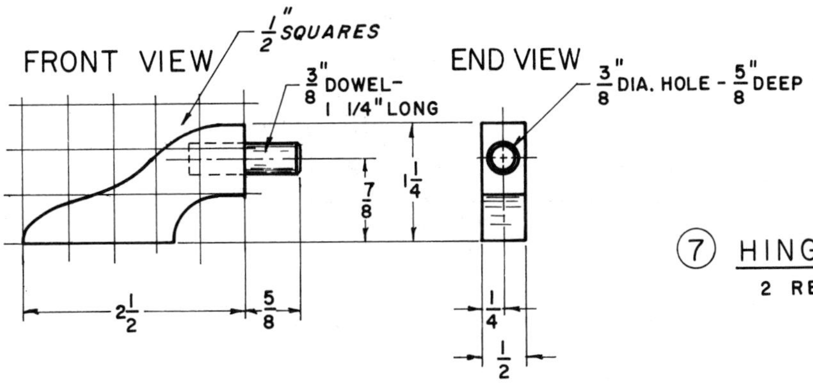
FRONT VIEW
1/2" SQUARES
3/8" DOWEL- 1 1/4" LONG
END VIEW
3/8" DIA. HOLE - 5/8" DEEP
7/8
1 1/4
2 1/2
5/8
1/4
1/2

⑦ HINGE SUPPORT

2 REQ'D

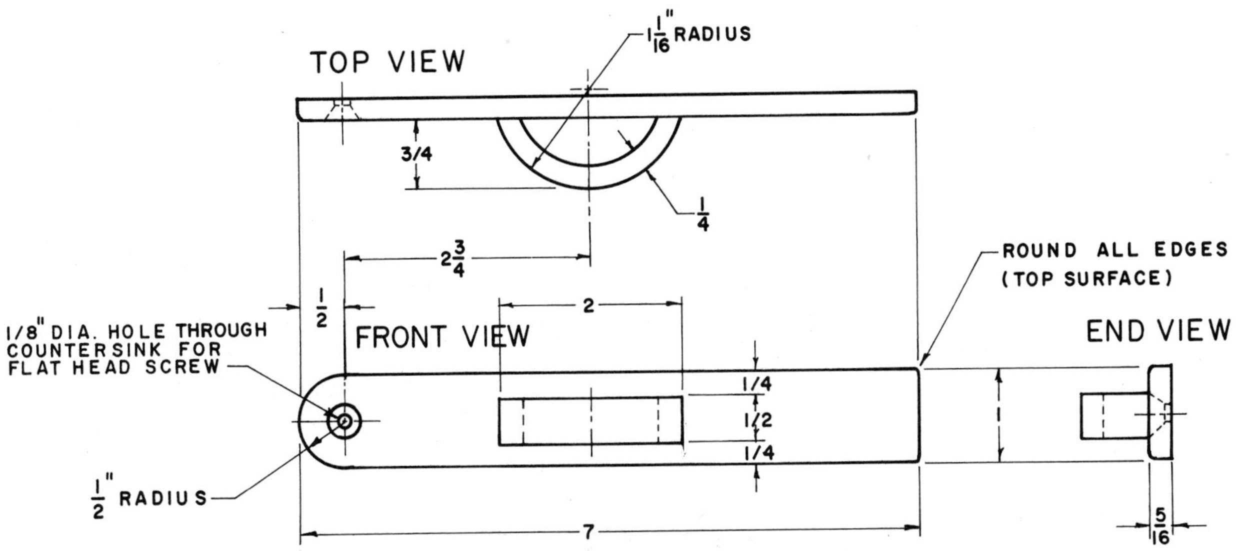
TOP VIEW
1 1/16" RADIUS
3/4
1/4
2 3/4
1/2
2
ROUND ALL EDGES (TOP SURFACE)
FRONT VIEW
END VIEW
1/8" DIA. HOLE THROUGH COUNTERSINK FOR FLAT HEAD SCREW
1/4
1/2
1/4
1/2" RADIUS
7
5/16

⑧ LATCH

1 REQ'D

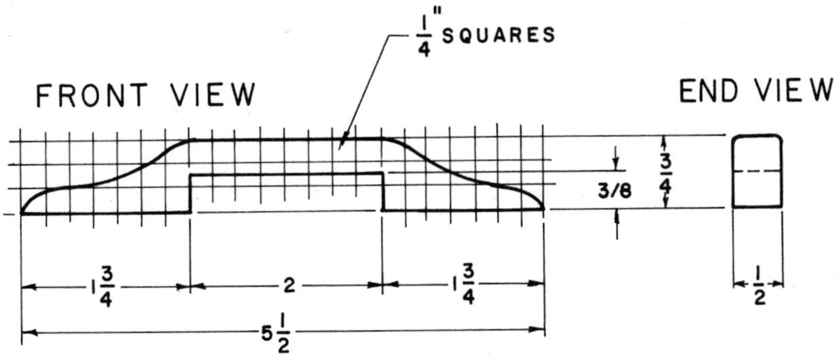
1/4" SQUARES
FRONT VIEW
END VIEW
3/8
3/4
1 3/4
2
1 3/4
5 1/2
1/2

⑨ LATCH GUIDE

1 REQ'D

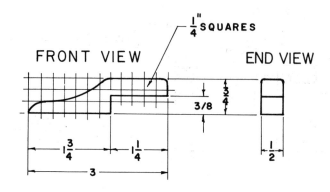

$\frac{1}{4}$" SQUARES

FRONT VIEW

END VIEW

$\frac{3}{4}$

3/8

$\frac{1}{2}$

$1\frac{3}{4}$ $1\frac{1}{4}$

3

⑩   LATCH STOP
1 REQ'D

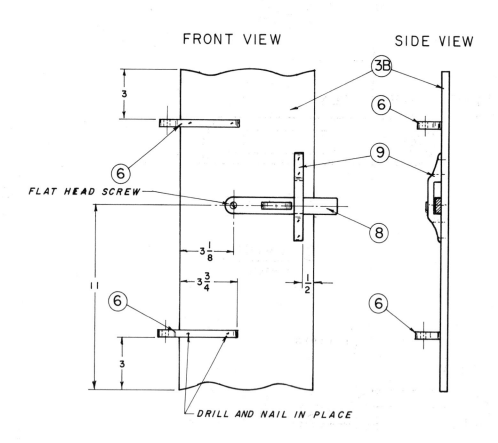

FRONT VIEW

SIDE VIEW

3

3B

6

6

9

FLAT HEAD SCREW

8

11

$3\frac{1}{8}$

$3\frac{3}{4}$

$\frac{1}{2}$

6

6

3

DRILL AND NAIL IN PLACE

⑪   SUBASSEMBLY
1 REQ'D

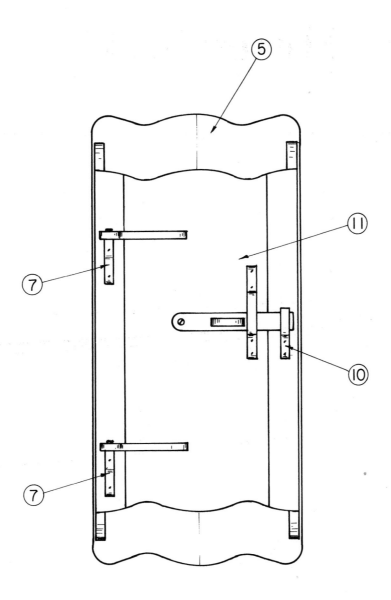

⑫   ASSEMBLY

Harvest Table

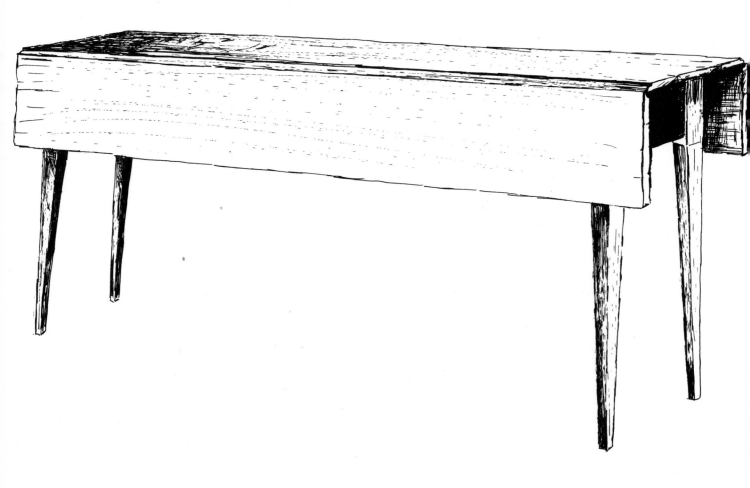

A focal point of activities for family gatherings at Thanksgiving and Christmas, this project will rapidly accumulate many fond memories. This harvest table is six feet long, but the dimensions could easily be shortened or lengthened to four or eight feet to suit your preference. The table design is pretty much standard for this period, combining simplicity with elegance and grace. When choosing the wood for the top boards, take time to find interesting grain patterns and flat, straight boards. The size of this particular table allows most chairs to fit under the table even when the leaves are down (when the table is not in use). Take care to position the back-flap hinges as indicated in the drawings, so that the leaves will function smoothly. Check to see that you have the proper equipment to cut the bead and cove as illustrated. It would be possible to make this project with simple straight edges in place of the bead and cove, but of course the table would not be authentic.

MATERIALS

(Recommended wood: cherry, walnut, butternut, maple, or pine)
two 2-by-2-inch 6-foot-long boards
three 1-by-5-inch 6-foot-long boards
one 1-by-2-inch 6-foot-long board
five 1-by-10-inch 6-foot-long boards
four back-flap hinges (special)
one ⅛-inch-diameter steel pin—12 inches long (to be cut into four 3-inch-long pieces)
one ¼-inch-diameter dowel—3 feet long
eight #10 flat head wood screws—1¼ inches long each
Water putty
Wood glue
Sandpaper—medium and fine
Tung oil
#0000 steel wool

INSTRUCTIONS

Cut the legs (figure 1) to length; then cut 2° tapers and mortises on both inside surfaces, as shown in the detail drawing. *Important:* the 2° taper is only on the two inside surfaces; the outside corners of the table should remain straight. Cut the supports (figures 2 and 3) to size and carefully cut the tenons to match the legs. Number the corners as you proceed; each mortise and tenon will custom-fit to size. Cut from scrap four of the corner braces, as shown in figure 5, and assemble. Drill holes and then glue and insert the ¼-inch dowels to pin the mortises and tenons together as shown—1 inch down and 2 inches apart. Cut and sand the ends smooth after the glue dries. Take care that the table stands level on the floor and is square at all corners. Cut up the ⅛-inch-diameter steel pin into four 3-inch-long pins. Drill and add as shown in figure 5. Check that the leaf supports function smoothly.

Glue up the material for the top board (figure 6). Be sure to stagger the direction of grain on each adjoining piece used to make up the top board. Square and cut the ends and sides. Cut the half-round bead as shown. Square and cut the ends and sides of the table leaves (figure 7) to size as shown in the detail drawing, and cut the half-round coves to fit the corresponding beads of the top board. Turn the top over and locate the spots where the four special back-flap hinges will be placed. Mark and chisel out space for the knuckle as shown on the assembly drawing (figure 8). *Important:* the knuckle must be placed up, as shown in the magnified view in figure 8, and must be located at the exact swing-point of the cove and bead radius. A regular hinge could be used, but would not give a smooth, even action. Screw the top subassembly to the leg subassembly by making simple securing blocks of suitable size from scrap wood. Check the action of the leaf supports. Adjust them if necessary by adding shims to the leaf supports, so that the top will sit flat and even when it is up.

FINISH

Sand all over and apply tung oil. (A light coat of stain may be applied before applying the tung oil, but it will look better over time if the wood is allowed to age by itself.) Apply two or three coats of tung oil, allowing the wood to dry thoroughly each time and sanding between coats with #0000 steel wool.

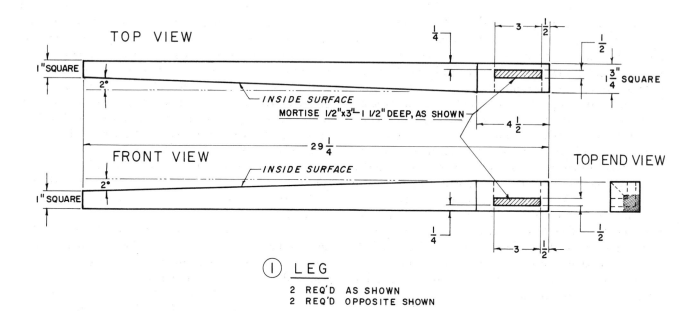

TOP VIEW

1" SQUARE

2°

INSIDE SURFACE

MORTISE 1/2"x3"- 1 1/2" DEEP, AS SHOWN

¼

3

½

½

1 3/4" SQUARE

FRONT VIEW

INSIDE SURFACE

29 1/4

4 1/2

TOP END VIEW

1" SQUARE

2°

¼

3

½

½

① LEG

2 REQ'D AS SHOWN
2 REQ'D OPPOSITE SHOWN

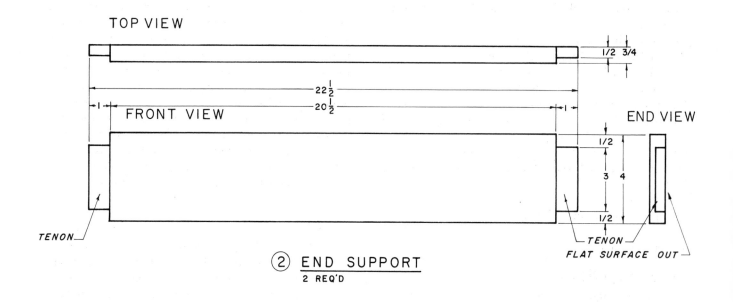

TOP VIEW

1/2 3/4

22 ½

20 ½

1

1

FRONT VIEW

END VIEW

1/2

3   4

1/2

TENON

TENON

FLAT SURFACE OUT

② END SUPPORT
2 REQ'D

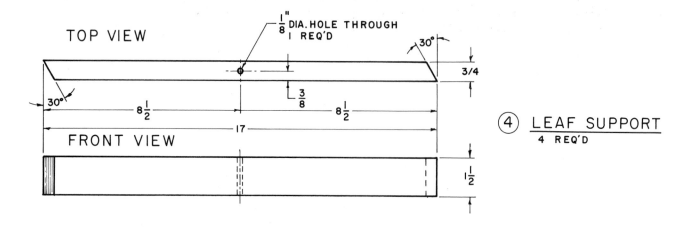

TOP VIEW

1/8" DIA. HOLE THROUGH
1 REQ'D

30°

3/4

30°

8 ½

3/8

8 ½

17

FRONT VIEW

1 ½

④ LEAF SUPPORT
4 REQ'D

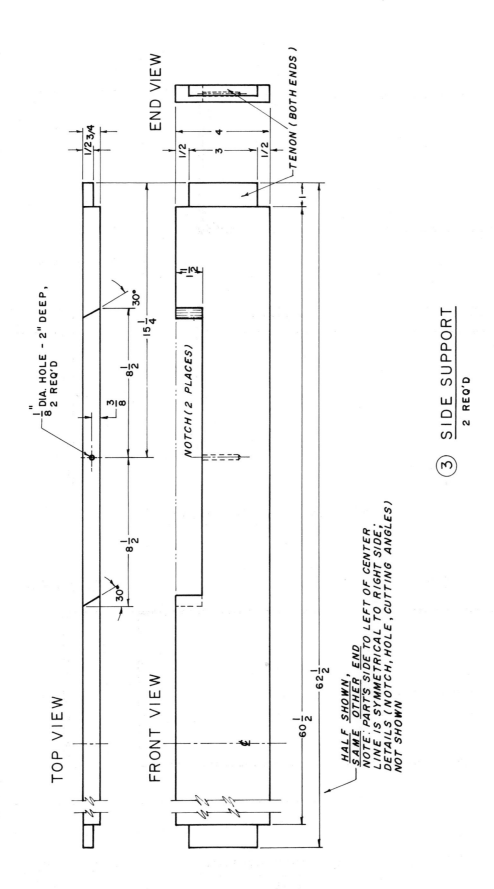

TOP VIEW

FRONT VIEW

END VIEW

$1 \frac{1}{2}$ DIA. HOLE - 2" DEEP, 2 REQ'D

30°

$15 \frac{1}{4}$

$8 \frac{1}{2}$

$\frac{3}{8}$

$8 \frac{1}{2}$

30°

NOTCH (2 PLACES)

$1 \frac{1}{2}$

TENON (BOTH ENDS)

4

$\frac{1}{2}$

3

$\frac{1}{2}$

1

$60 \frac{1}{2}$

$62 \frac{1}{2}$

$1 2 \frac{3}{4}$

HALF SHOWN, END SAME OTHER. END
NOTE: PART'S SIDE TO LEFT OF CENTER LINE IS SYMMETRICAL TO RIGHT SIDE; DETAILS (NOTCH, HOLE, CUTTING ANGLES) NOT SHOWN

(3) SIDE SUPPORT
2 REQ'D

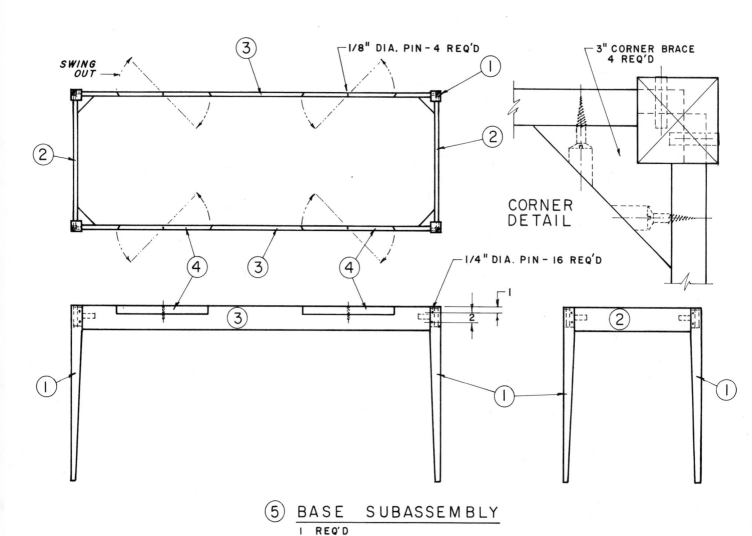

SWING OUT →

③

1/8" DIA. PIN - 4 REQ'D

①

②

②

④   ③   ④

3" CORNER BRACE
4 REQ'D

CORNER
DETAIL

1/4" DIA. PIN - 16 REQ'D

③

①

①

②

①

⑤ BASE   SUBASSEMBLY
I REQ'D

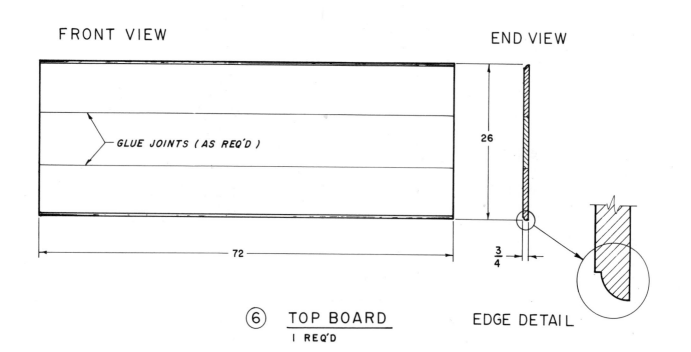

FRONT VIEW

END VIEW

GLUE JOINTS (AS REQ'D)

26

72

3/4

⑥   TOP BOARD
I REQ'D

EDGE DETAIL

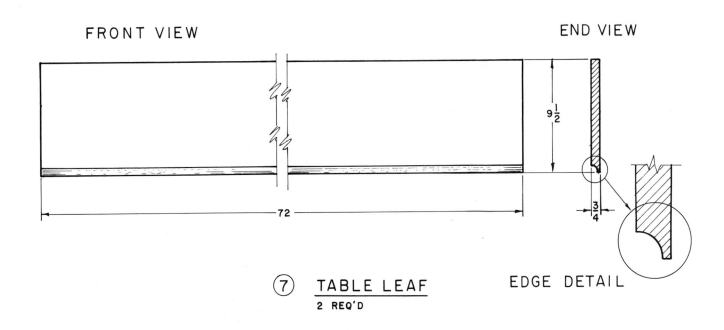

FRONT VIEW

END VIEW

9½

72

¾

⑦ TABLE LEAF
2 REQ'D

EDGE DETAIL

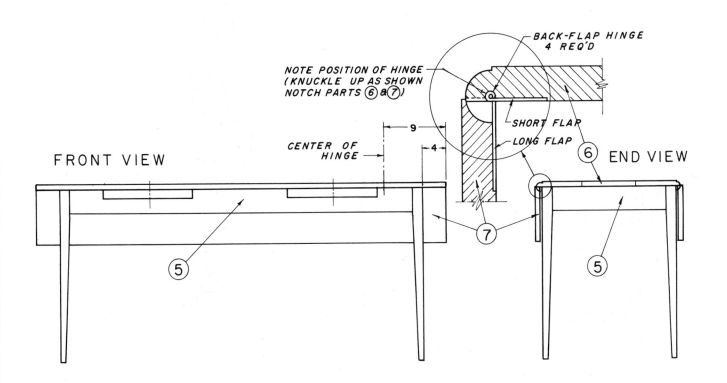

BACK-FLAP HINGE
4 REQ'D

NOTE POSITION OF HINGE
(KNUCKLE UP AS SHOWN
NOTCH PARTS ⑥ & ⑦)

SHORT FLAP
LONG FLAP

CENTER OF
HINGE

9

4

FRONT VIEW

⑥ END VIEW

⑤

⑦

⑤

⑧ ASSEMBLY

Cradle

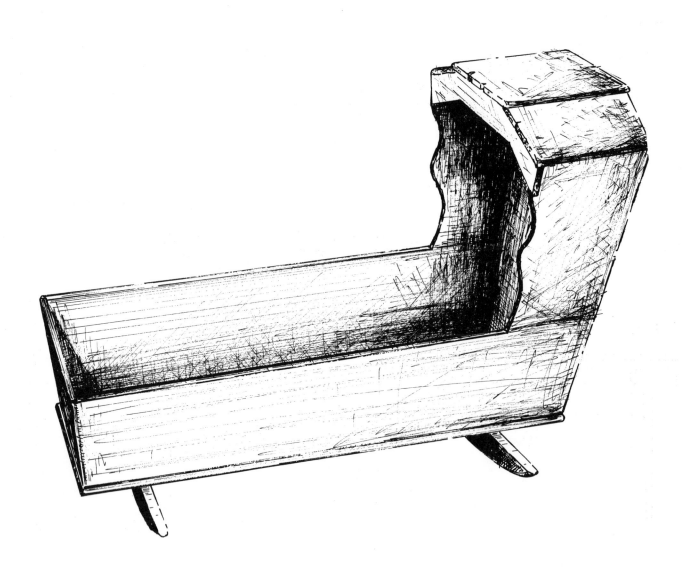

The original cradle of this design was found in southern New Hampshire. Although it is probably a one-of-a-kind model, it does follow the traditional lines of cradles made around 1780 in New England. At the time, people thought that the night air brought on lung disorders; therefore, cradles were made with solid sides and hoods to ward off drafts. The baby surely was well protected in this model. It was also believed that the motion of the rockers actually relieved colic. Most cradles were made of easy-to-work pine or poplar. This cradle would make a nice display for an antique doll collection, or a good planter, or perhaps a magazine rack.

MATERIALS

(Recommended wood: pine)
one 5/4-by-8-inch 6-foot-long board
one 5/4-by-4-inch 4-foot-long board
two 1-by-10-inch 10-foot-long boards
one 3/8-by-10-inch 4-foot-long board
one 1/4-inch-diameter dowel—3 feet long
twenty-four small square-cut nails
Water putty
Wood glue
Sandpaper—medium and fine
Stain of your choice
Tung oil
Wash

INSTRUCTIONS

Glue up material for the base and base wing (figures 1 and 6). Let the glue set, and cut the parts slightly oversize. Carefully locate and cut the two notches in the base, as shown. Cut to size the rockers (figure 2). Lay out and cut to size the sides (figure 3). Notice that one side is cut as shown; the other, opposite the way shown. Do not drill the two 1/4-inch holes through the sides and side wing tenons at this time. Lay out and cut to size the side wings (figure 4). Cut the tenons to fit the mortises in the sides (figure 3). Drill the two 1/4-inch-diameter holes at assembly, as shown in figure 5, and add the 1/4-inch-diameter dowels. Notice that there are left and right side subassemblies which mirror each other. Cut the foot ends (figure 7) at an angle of 4° as shown. Cut the support (figure 8) as shown in the detail plan. The pictured roof side (figure 9) is shown at its approximate shape and size; both roof sides must be fitted at final assembly. Cut to size the roof center (figure 10), and round its ends per the detail drawing. Dry-fit all parts, and trim them to fit before gluing and nailing them together. Be sure that the roof sides are parallel to the back wing (figure 6) and that they blend into the side wings as shown in the assembly drawing.

FINISH

Sand all over, distress to suit, and resand. Apply stain and tung oil, apply the wash coat, allow everything to dry, and apply a final coat of tung oil.

TOP VIEW

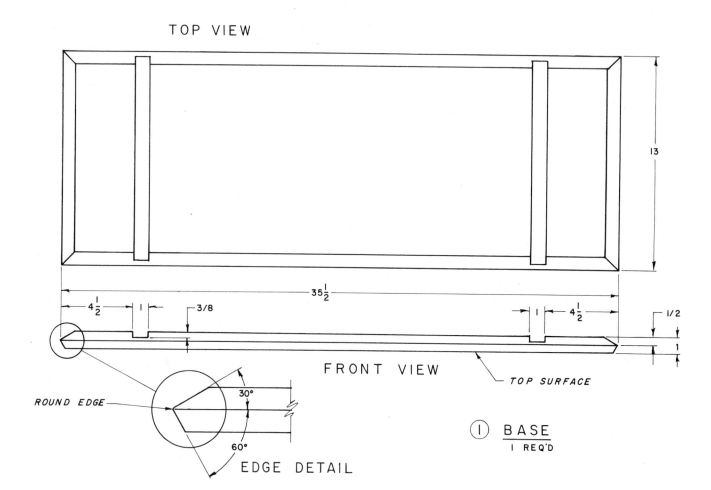

13

35 1/2

4 1/2   1   3/8   1   4 1/2   1/2

FRONT VIEW

TOP SURFACE

ROUND EDGE

30°

60°

EDGE DETAIL

① BASE
1 REQ'D

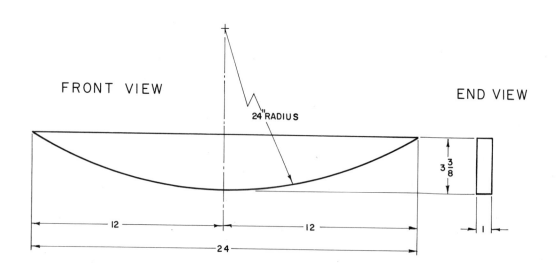

FRONT VIEW

24" RADIUS

END VIEW

3 3/8

12   12

24   1

② ROCKERS
2 REQ'D

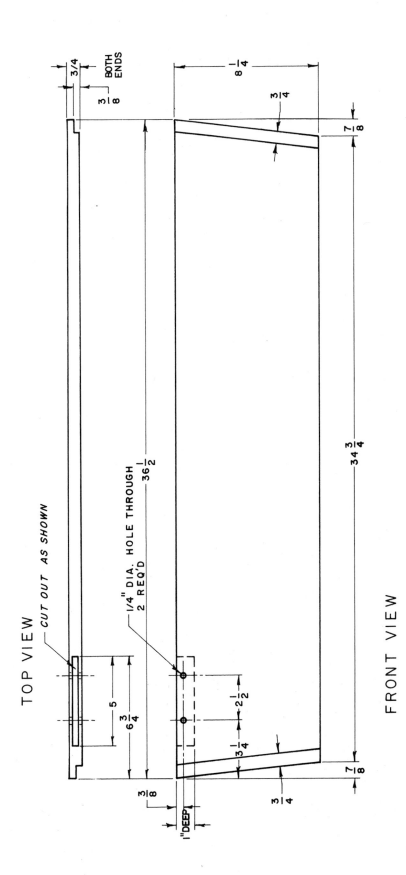

TOP VIEW

CUT OUT AS SHOWN

3/4

BOTH ENDS

$\frac{3}{8}$

1/4" DIA. HOLE THROUGH
2 REQ'D

$36\frac{1}{2}$

5

$6\frac{3}{4}$

$8\frac{1}{4}$

$\frac{3}{4}$

$\frac{7}{8}$

$34\frac{3}{4}$

$2\frac{1}{2}$

$3\frac{1}{4}$

$\frac{7}{8}$

$\frac{3}{4}$

$\frac{3}{8}$

1" DEEP

FRONT VIEW

③ SIDE
1 REQ'D   AS SHOWN
1 REQ'D   OPPOSITE SHOWN

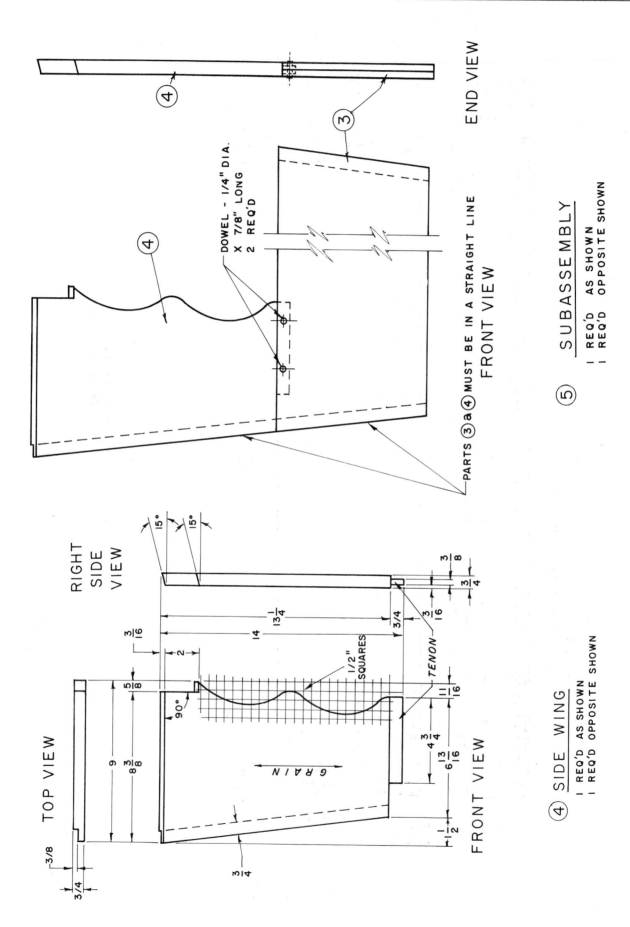

END VIEW

④

③

DOWEL – 1/4" DIA.
X 7/8" LONG
2 REQ'D

④

PARTS ③ & ④ MUST BE IN A STRAIGHT LINE
FRONT VIEW

⑤ SUBASSEMBLY

I REQ'D   AS SHOWN
I REQ'D   OPPOSITE SHOWN

RIGHT
SIDE
VIEW

15° 15°

TOP VIEW

3/8

3/4

3/16

5/8

9

8 3/8

90°

2

13 1/4

14

1/2" SQUARES

GRAIN

3 1/16

3/4

TENON

3/8

3/4

11/16

4 3/4

13/16

6 16

1 1/2

3 1/4

FRONT VIEW

④ SIDE WING

I REQ'D   AS SHOWN
I REQ'D   OPPOSITE SHOWN

SIDE VIEW

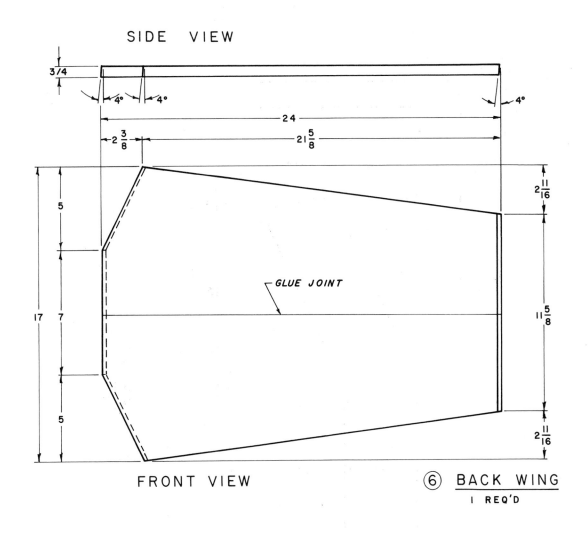

3/4

4° 4° 4°

24

2 3/8 21 5/8

2 11/16

5

17 7 11 5/8

GLUE JOINT

5

2 11/16

FRONT VIEW ⑥ BACK WING
1 REQ'D

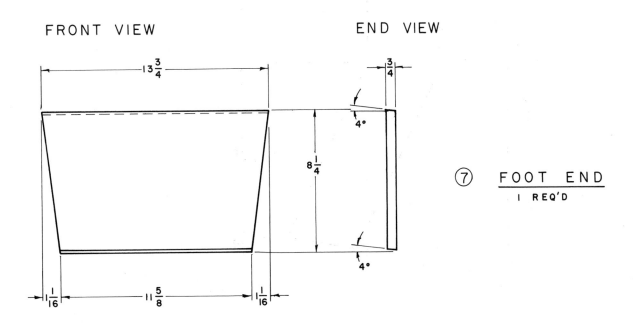

FRONT VIEW END VIEW

13 3/4 3/4

4°

8 1/4

⑦ FOOT END
1 REQ'D

4°

1 1/16 11 5/8 1 1/16

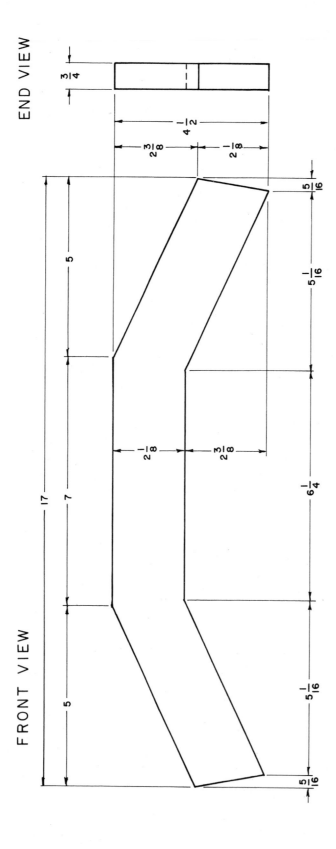

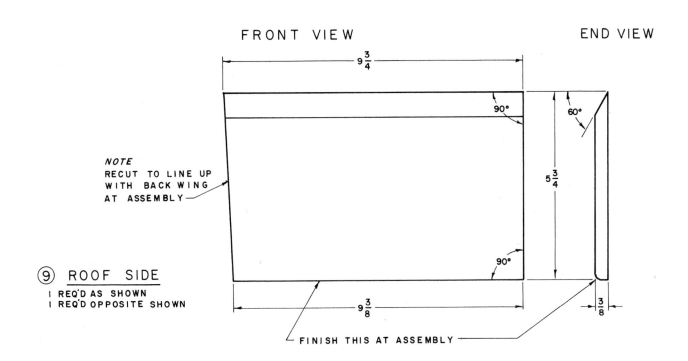

FRONT VIEW   END VIEW

$9\frac{3}{4}$

90°

60°

$5\frac{3}{4}$

NOTE
RECUT TO LINE UP
WITH BACK WING
AT ASSEMBLY

90°

⑨ ROOF SIDE
1 REQ'D AS SHOWN
1 REQ'D OPPOSITE SHOWN

$9\frac{3}{8}$

$\frac{3}{8}$

└ FINISH THIS AT ASSEMBLY ┘

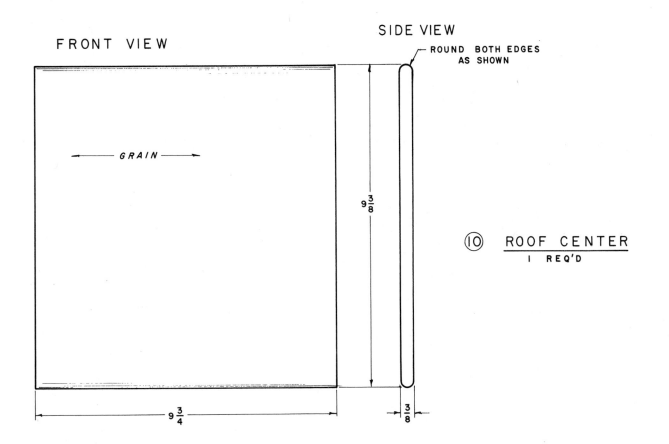

FRONT VIEW   SIDE VIEW

ROUND BOTH EDGES
AS SHOWN

GRAIN

$9\frac{3}{8}$

⑩ ROOF CENTER
1 REQ'D

$9\frac{3}{4}$

$\frac{3}{8}$

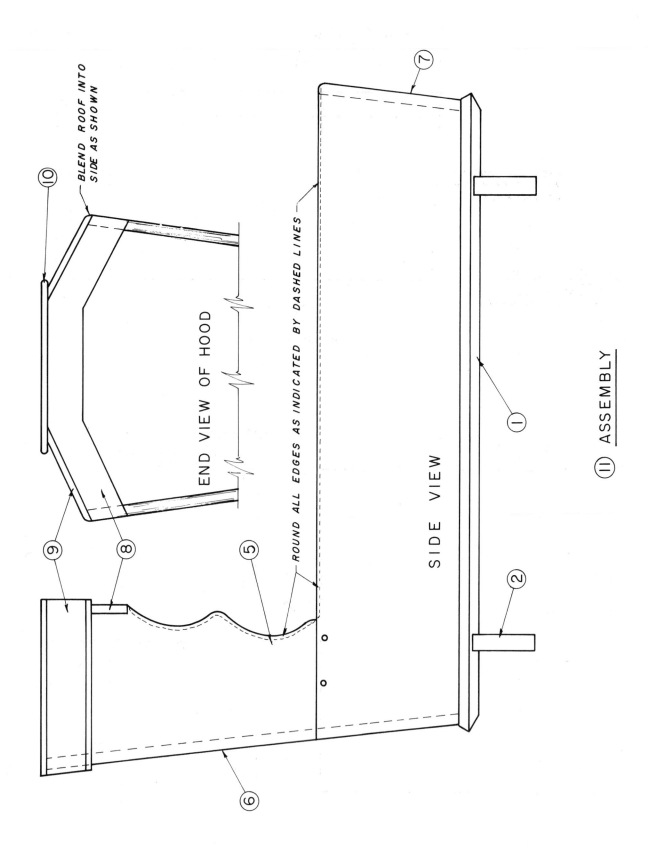

END VIEW OF HOOD

BLEND ROOF INTO SIDE AS SHOWN

ROUND ALL EDGES AS INDICATED BY DASHED LINES

SIDE VIEW

⑪ ASSEMBLY

Quick and Easy Washer

Washing was an all-day project back before this "modern" quick and easy washer was manufactured. This project is by far the newest item in this book, but because it is unique it has been included. Before the advent of this innovative washer, women had to tote water from the spring behind their house, heat it over an open flame, and scrub the clothes on a corrugated scrub board made of hardwood. Today, thanks to these plans, the modern women can enjoy the ease of this quick and easy washer and will probably be forever grateful to you for constructing it for her. This model was commercially manufactured in the late 1800s and early 1900s and probably was sold through mail-order catalogs. Today, other than for an occasional wash, it can be put to use as a planter or flower container, and of course it has considerable conversation value. If you plan to stencil it to match the original, you should borrow a book on the subject from a local library.

MATERIALS

(Recommended wood: spruce or pine, *with oak* as indicated)
two 1-by-8-inch 10-foot-long boards
one 1-by-4-inch 6-foot-long board
one 1-inch-diameter dowel—3 feet long
one ¾-inch-diameter dowel—3 feet long
two 1-by-4-inch 6-foot-long boards (oak)
one 1-by-2-inch 6-foot-long board (oak)
one 24-by-48-inch light-gauge steel sheet
twenty-four sixpenny common nails
eight ¼-inch-diameter stove bolts—¾ inches long, with washers and square nuts
Water putty
Wood glue
Sandpaper—medium and fine
Antique red paint and black paint
Stencil material
Tung oil

INSTRUCTIONS

Glue up material for the side boards (figure 1), and cut them to size in accordance with the detail plans. Notch and drill all holes as indicated. Any kind of wood could be used, but to be authentic the legs (figure 2) should be cut from a piece of oak.

These are not painted; they are left clear, with only three or four coats of tung oil covering them. Cut to size the remainder of the washing trough (figures 3, 4, 5, 6, and 7). Sand all over and assemble the shelves and support blocks (figures 6 and 7), as shown in figure 8. Glue and nail together the side, end, and center boards (figures 1, 3, and 4). Turn this piece over and tape a piece of cardboard, approximately 2 feet by 4 feet, in place at the bottom, then make an accurate template of the exact size and shape of the bottom (figure 5). Do not forget to add the ¼-inch tabs to the outside of the pattern, as shown. Make notches approximately ½ inch apart as shown.

Transfer the template to a sheet of light-gauge metal and cut the shape out. Cut the piece a little long, and trim it to size at assembly. Tack the bottom in place and fold the tabs over, taking care that all sharp edges are bent over and sanded smooth. Temporarily bolt the legs in place, using the ¼-inch-diameter stove bolts, washers, and nuts. Check to see that the subassembly sits flat on the floor without rocking. Trim the leg bottoms if necessary to accomplish this.

Cut to size the scrubber sides, arms, and ribs (figures 10, 11, and 12), and assemble them as shown in figure 13. Notice that the scrubber arms (figure 11) should be made of oak and should not be painted.

FINISH

Paint the subassembly dull black, and allow it to dry. Remove the legs, paint the body antique red, and allow it to dry. Coat the legs and scrubber arms with three or four coats of tung oil; these parts should be high-gloss and natural.

Enlarge the stencil pattern and cut it out of stencil material. Apply the design to the body. Allow this to dry, and bolt the legs permanently in place.

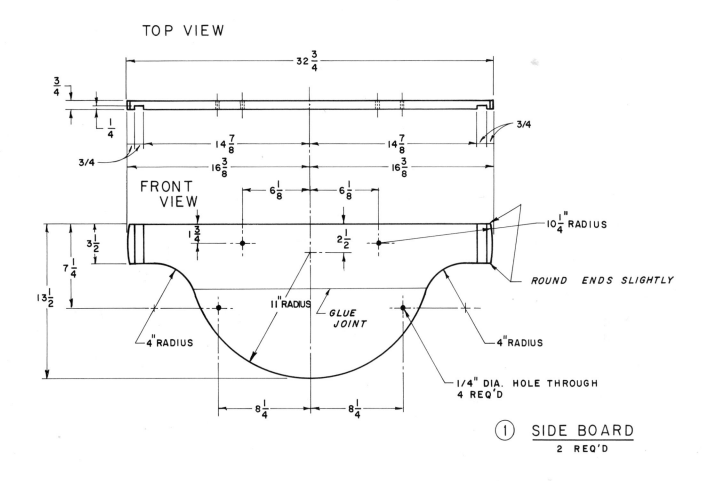

TOP VIEW

FRONT VIEW

① SIDE BOARD
2 REQ'D

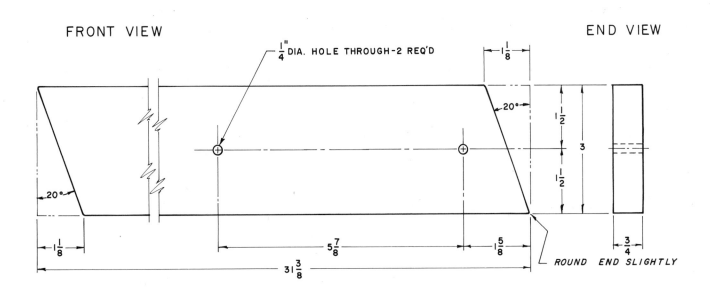

FRONT VIEW

END VIEW

② LEG
4 REQ'D

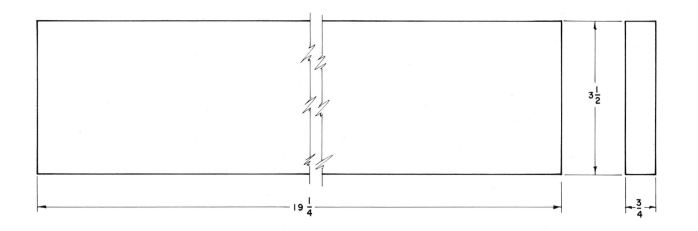

FRONT VIEW   END VIEW

$3\frac{1}{2}$

$19\frac{1}{4}$

$\frac{3}{4}$

③ END BOARD
2 REQ'D

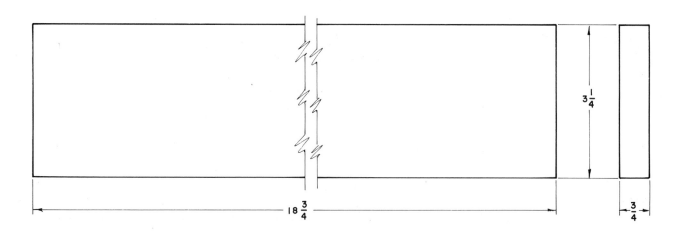

FRONT VIEW   END VIEW

$3\frac{1}{4}$

$18\frac{3}{4}$

$\frac{3}{4}$

④ CENTER BOARD
1 REQ'D

FRONT VIEW

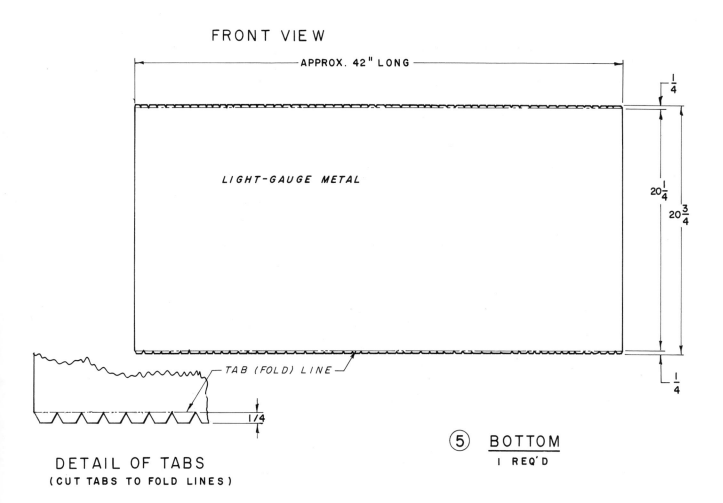

APPROX. 42" LONG

LIGHT-GAUGE METAL

$\frac{1}{4}$

$20\frac{1}{4}$

$20\frac{3}{4}$

$\frac{1}{4}$

TAB (FOLD) LINE

$1/4$

DETAIL OF TABS
(CUT TABS TO FOLD LINES)

⑤ BOTTOM
1 REQ'D

FRONT VIEW   END VIEW

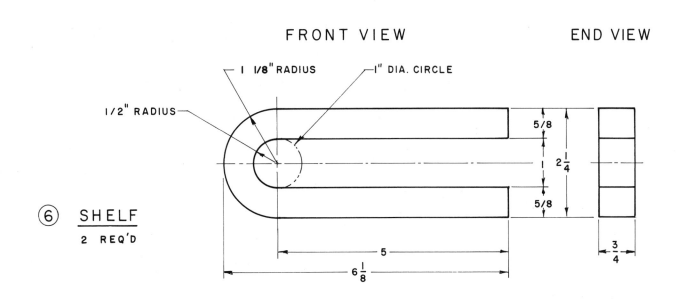

1 1/8" RADIUS   1" DIA. CIRCLE

1/2" RADIUS

5/8

$2\frac{1}{4}$

5/8

⑥ SHELF
2 REQ'D

5

$6\frac{1}{8}$

$\frac{3}{4}$

FRONT VIEW

END VIEW

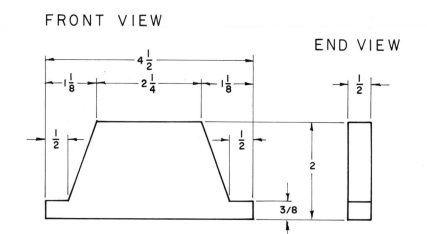

⑦ SUPPORT BLOCK
2 REQ'D

FRONT VIEW   END VIEW

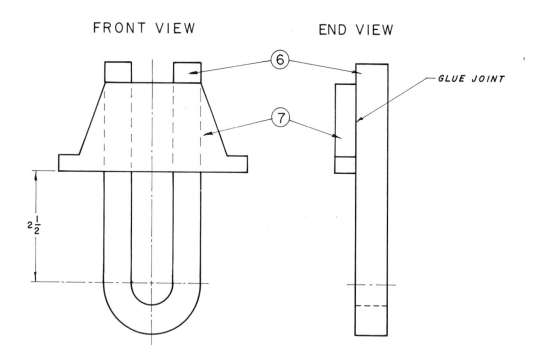

⑧   SUBASSEMBLY
2 REQ'D

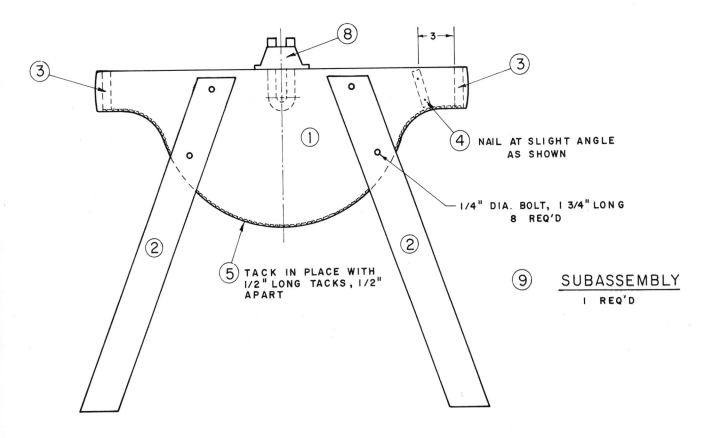

③

⑧

③

3

④ NAIL AT SLIGHT ANGLE
AS SHOWN

1/4" DIA. BOLT, 1 3/4" LONG
8 REQ'D

①

② ②

⑤ TACK IN PLACE WITH
1/2" LONG TACKS, 1/2"
APART

⑨ <u>SUBASSEMBLY</u>
1 REQ'D

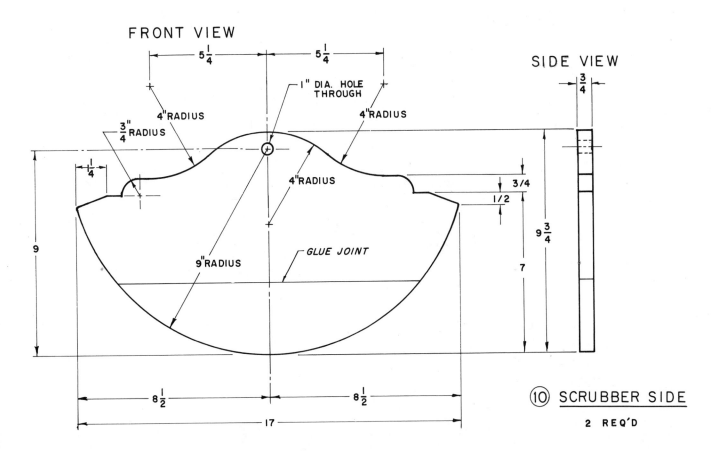

FRONT VIEW

5 1/4   5 1/4

1" DIA. HOLE
THROUGH

4"RADIUS

4"RADIUS

3/4"RADIUS

1/4

4"RADIUS

9"RADIUS

GLUE JOINT

9

8 1/2   8 1/2

17

SIDE VIEW

3/4

3/4

1/2

9 3/4

7

⑩ <u>SCRUBBER SIDE</u>
2 REQ'D

FRONT VIEW   END VIEW

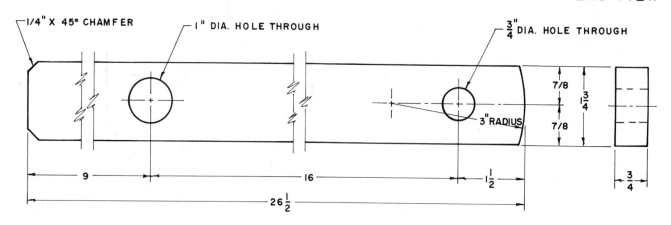

1/4" X 45° CHAMFER   I" DIA. HOLE THROUGH   3/4" DIA. HOLE THROUGH

7/8   1 3/4   7/8

3" RADIUS

9   16   1 1/2   3/4

26 1/2

⑪ SCRUBBER ARM
2 REQ'D

FRONT VIEW   END VIEW

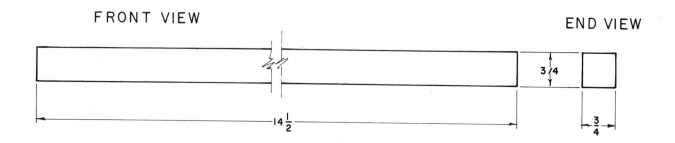

3/4

14 1/2   3/4

⑫ SCRUBBER RIB
10 REQ'D

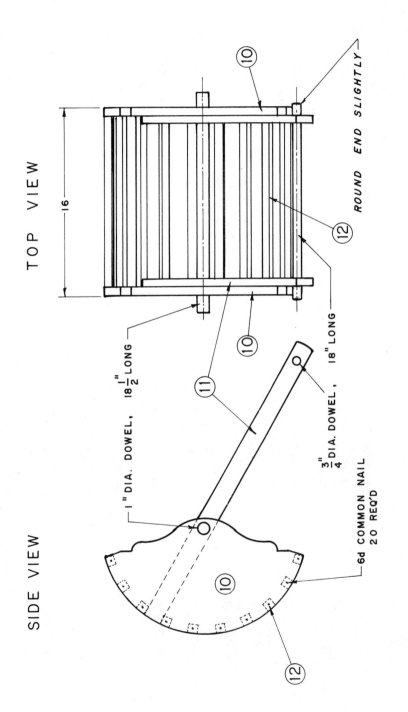

TOP VIEW

16

ROUND END SLIGHTLY

SIDE VIEW

1" DIA. DOWEL, $18\frac{1}{2}$" LONG

$\frac{3}{4}$" DIA. DOWEL, 18" LONG

6d COMMON NAIL
20 REQ'D

⑬ SUBASSEMBLY
1 REQ'D

1/2" SQUARES

1/2" SQUARES

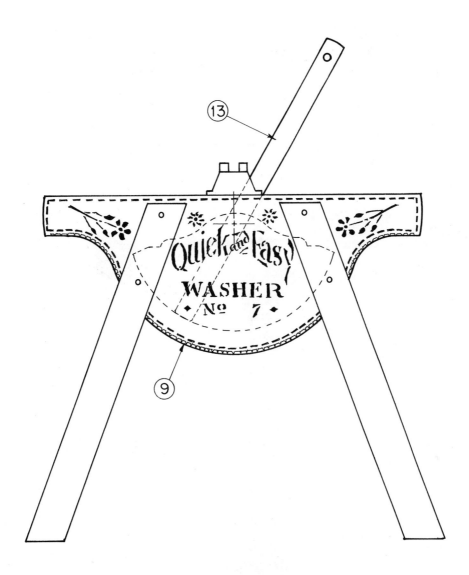

⑭   ASSEMBLY

Candle Stand

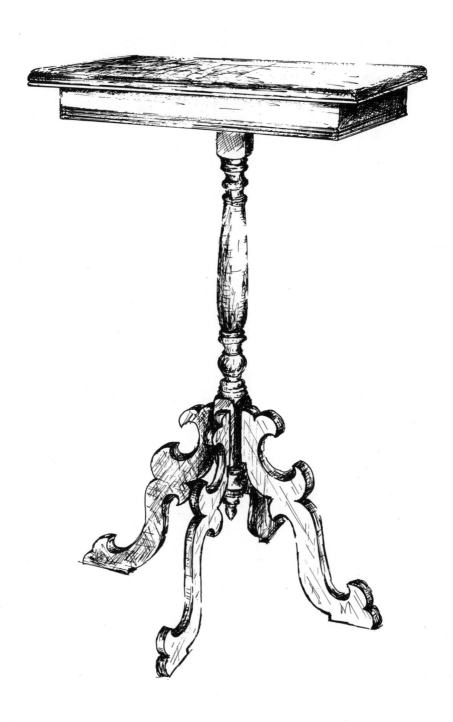

This Victorian-style candle stand was probably factory-made between 1880 and 1900. The original was found piece-by-piece in northern Vermont, as the snow of winter melted into spring. Evidently, it had been badly broken and simply thrown out into the field not to be found until spring. Heaven knows how long it had been out in the field. Every other day or so another piece would be found, and (with some luck) the entire stand emerged.

The original is made of oak, which is very porous and must be filled to achieve a smooth finish.

MATERIALS

(Recommended wood: oak)
one 1-by-4-inch 5-foot-long board
one 1½-by-1½-inch 3-foot-long board
one 1-by-8-inch 3-foot-long board
one ⁵⁄₁₆-by-2-inch 5-foot-long board
one 1-by-3-inch 1-foot-long piece of *pine* scrap for top support
one ¼-inch-diameter dowel—3 feet long
two #10 flat head wood screws—1¼ inches long each
thirty square-cut nails to suit
Water putty
Wood glue
Grain filler
Sandpaper—medium and fine
Dark oak stain
Tung oil

INSTRUCTIONS

Carefully make a cardboard pattern of the legs (figure 1), using ½-inch squares as illustrated on the detail plan. Line up the pattern on the wood, taking care that the grain is going in the right direction, and cut the shape out. If possible, tack or tape all four legs together and cut and sand them while they are together so that they will all be exactly the same size. Do not round the edges; double-check that you are holding the 90° angle as illustrated. Turn the center stem (figure 2) as shown in the detail drawing. Oak is stringy and hard to turn, so be especially careful in turning it. The two very small diameters require the most care of all.

Cut to size the top (figure 3), and shape the edges as shown in the detail drawing. Sand, and set it aside for now. It is a good idea to cut the molding grooves down the full 5-foot length of molding material, before cutting it apart to size as shown in figures 4 and 5. Assemble the top and moldings as illustrated in figure 6. Cut the top supports (figure 7) from a scrap piece of pine, and attach it to the bottom surface of the top subassembly (figure 6) with the two wood screws. Be sure the ¾-inch hole is at the exact center of the top subassembly. Glue and clamp the legs to the main stem. When the glue is dry, check to see that the assembly stands flat without rocking. Trim the legs, if necessary.

FINISH

Sand all over and apply a commercial wood filler, following the suggested instructions on the can. Resand and apply stain. Apply tung oil to suit.

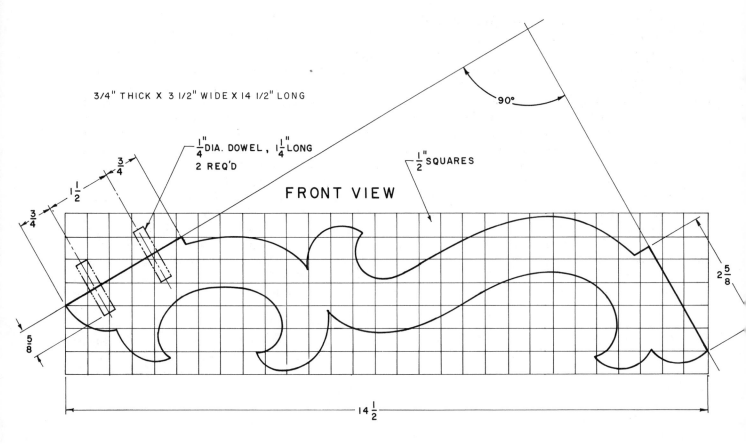

3/4" THICK X 3 1/2" WIDE X 14 1/2" LONG

$\frac{1}{4}$" DIA. DOWEL , $1\frac{1}{4}$" LONG
2 REQ'D

$\frac{3}{4}$

$1\frac{1}{2}$

$\frac{3}{4}$

$\frac{5}{8}$

FRONT VIEW

$\frac{1}{2}$" SQUARES

90°

$2\frac{5}{8}$

$14\frac{1}{2}$

① LEG
4 REQ'D

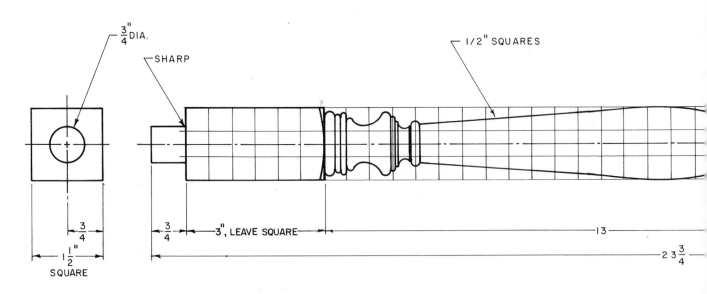

$\frac{3}{4}$" DIA.

SHARP

1/2" SQUARES

$\frac{3}{4}$

$\frac{3}{4}$

3", LEAVE SQUARE

13

$23\frac{3}{4}$

$1\frac{1}{2}$"
SQUARE

END VIEW

SIDE VIEW

TOP VIEW

END VIEW

GLUE JOINT

14

16 3/4

EDGE DETAIL

3/4

3/8

3/16

(3) TOP
1 REQ'D

1 1/2

1/4" DIA. HOLE - *DRILL TO MATCH LEG (PART ①)*
THROUGH
2 REQ'D EACH SIDE

3 5/8", LEAVE SQUARE

3 3/8"

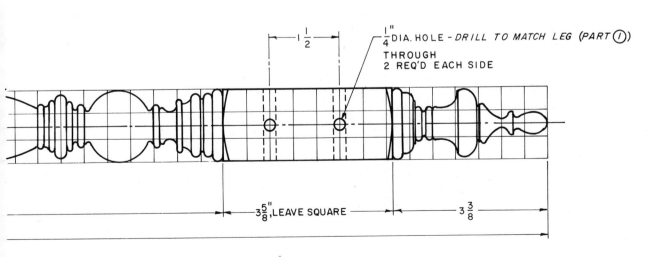

(2) STEM CENTER
1 REQ'D

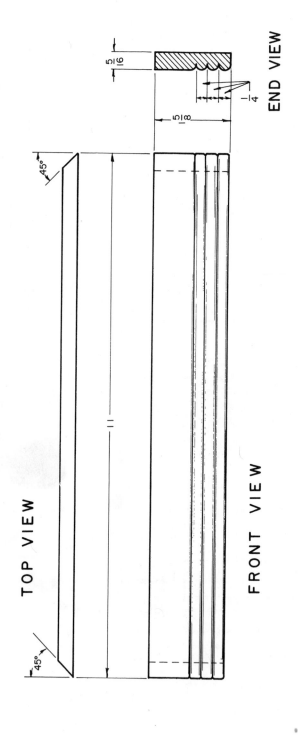

TOP VIEW

45°

45°

11

FRONT VIEW

5/16

5/8

END VIEW

1/4

SIDE MOLDING
2 REQ'D

④

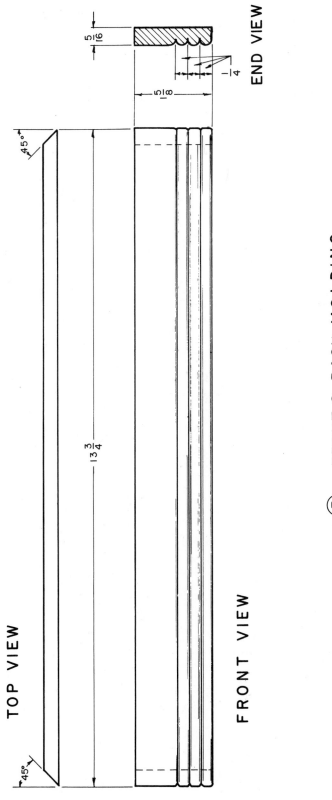

TOP VIEW

45°

45°

13 3/4

FRONT VIEW

5/16

5/8

1/4

END VIEW

⑤ FRONT & BACK MOLDING

2 REQ'D

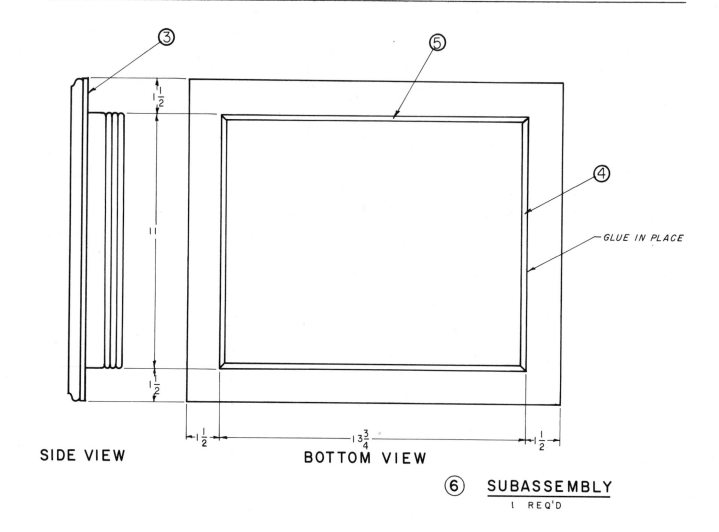

SIDE VIEW   BOTTOM VIEW

⑥ SUBASSEMBLY
    I REQ'D

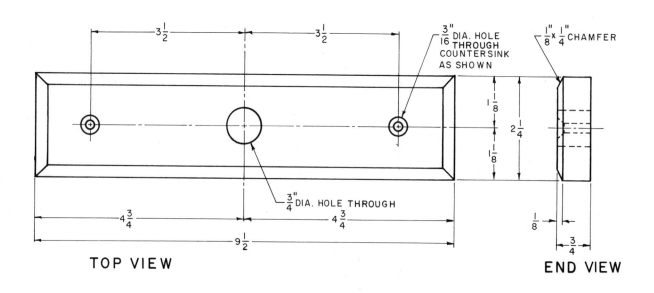

TOP VIEW   END VIEW

⑦ TOP SUPPORT
    I REQ'D

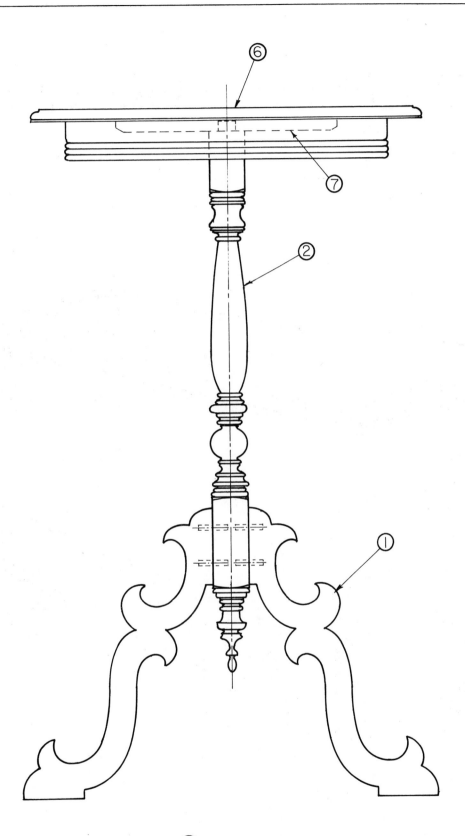

⑧ <u>ASSEMBLY</u>

One-Drawer Blanket Chest

Blanket chests were very popular from the early 1700s to around 1850. This particular chest was made about the year 1800. The original—like most—was made of very wide pine boards (although some were made of maple), and it was painted a very old-style greenish blue color. Some blanket chests had a painted grain for added elegance. Before starting this project, check the overall size. This is a very large blanket chest—in fact, it may be the largest blanket chest I have ever seen. Make sure that you have room for such a large piece of furniture. The original chest had a compartment made especially for candles, built into the interior of the chest.

MATERIALS

(Recommended wood: pine)
five 1-by-12-inch 12-foot-long boards
one ½-by-12-inch 10-foot-long board
one 1-by-8-inch 8-foot-long board
two ½-by-8-inch 8-foot-long boards
thirty-six square-cut nails (old if possible) to suit
two 2¼-inch-diameter wooden knobs
two 2-inch-long brass hinges
Water putty
Wood glue
Sandpaper—medium and fine
Stain or paint of your choice
Tung oil
Wash

INSTRUCTIONS

Cut all parts to size as specified in the individual detail drawings, taking care that everything is square. Assemble them as shown in figure 8. Glue and nail them together, but do not try to hide the square-cut nails. Predrill pilot holes for the legs, drawer spacers, and front spaces (figures 5, 6, and 7), so that these do not split during nailing. Glue and clamp the top board (figure 9) as shown in the detail drawings. You may have to nail the ½-inch-thick boards to the ¾-inch-thick boards with small finish nails; if so, nail at an angle and countersink and fill these nail holes with wood putty. Round the front and side top edge as shown.

Cut to size the drawer parts (figures 11, 12, 13, and 14). Notice the odd trim at the drawer bottom (figure 14). This unusual cut was used a lot on furniture drawers of this particular period. Keep all cuts square and dry-fit all parts. Make sure the drawer front (figure 11) is an exact fit with the main subassembly. After checking for size and fit, glue and nail the drawer subassembly together. Do not nail or glue the bottom board (figure 14) in place—let it float. Check that the drawer fits and slides into the main subassembly. Sand to fit, if necessary.

FINISH

Fill with water putty and sand all over. Distress and add "wear" surfaces or edges to the top and drawer front to suit. Resand, and apply a coat of tung oil and two coats of the paint of your choice. To add a very old look, sand away paint at all the "worn" edges—for example, along the top edge of the drawer or wherever you think the paint would have worn with years of use. Apply a coat of wash and allow to dry. Apply a final coat of tung oil.

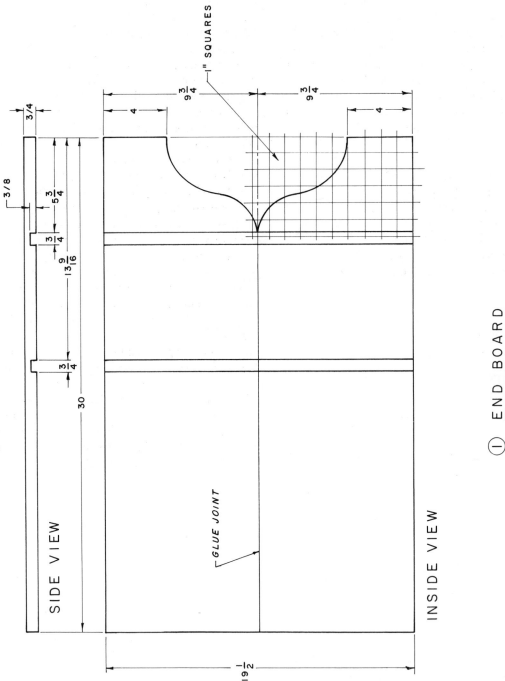

SIDE VIEW

INSIDE VIEW

① END BOARD
2 REQ'D

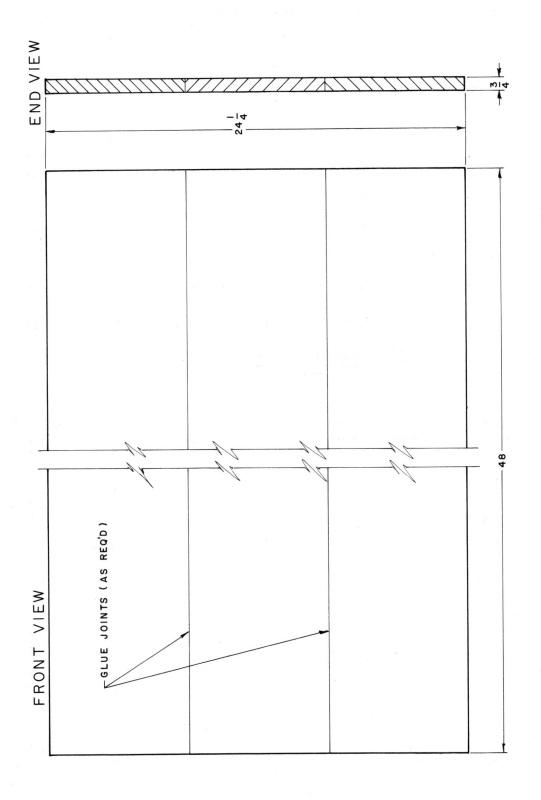

END VIEW

$24\frac{1}{4}$

$\frac{3}{4}$

FRONT VIEW

GLUE JOINTS (AS REQ'D)

48

② BACK BOARD
1 REQ'D

FRONT VIEW

END VIEW

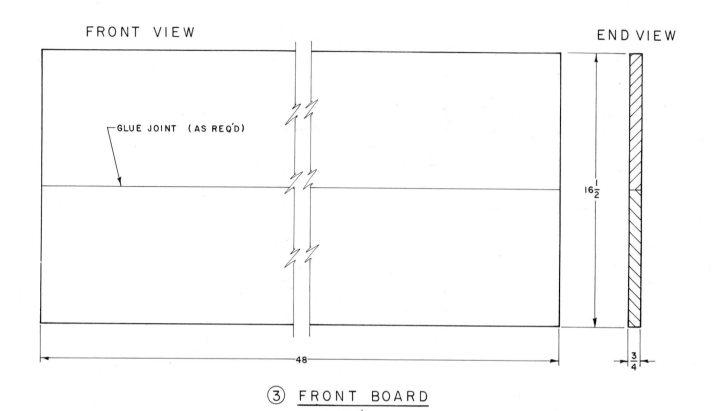

GLUE JOINT (AS REQ'D)

$16\frac{1}{2}$

48

$\frac{3}{4}$

③ FRONT BOARD
1 REQ'D

FRONT VIEW

END VIEW

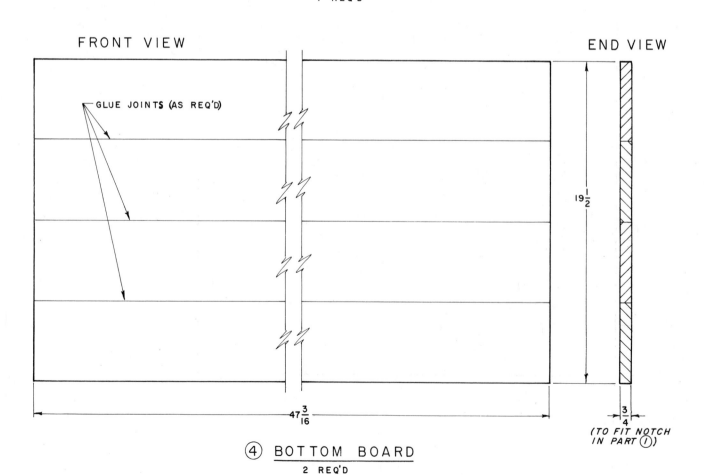

GLUE JOINTS (AS REQ'D)

$19\frac{1}{2}$

$47\frac{3}{16}$

$\frac{3}{4}$

(TO FIT NOTCH
IN PART ①)

④ BOTTOM BOARD
2 REQ'D

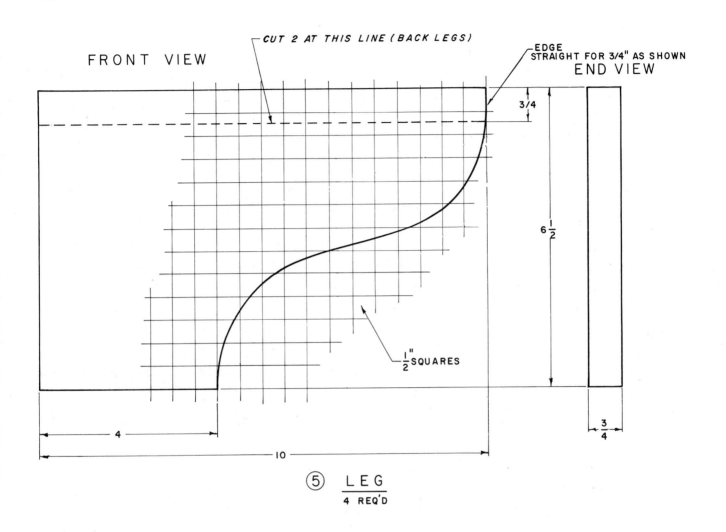

CUT 2 AT THIS LINE (BACK LEGS)

FRONT VIEW

EDGE
STRAIGHT FOR 3/4" AS SHOWN
END VIEW

3/4

$6\frac{1}{2}$

$\frac{1}{2}$" SQUARES

4

10

$\frac{3}{4}$

⑤ <u>L E G</u>
4 REQ'D

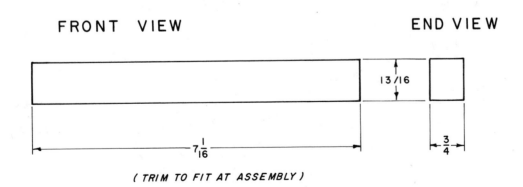

FRONT VIEW

END VIEW

13/16

$7\frac{1}{16}$

$\frac{3}{4}$

(TRIM TO FIT AT ASSEMBLY)

⑥ DRAWER SPACER
2 REQ'D

FRONT VIEW

END VIEW

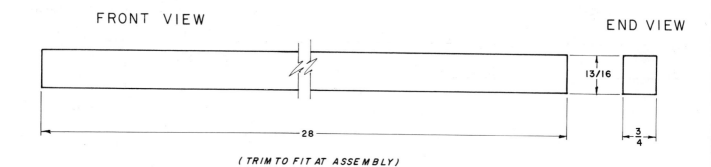

13/16

28

3/4

(TRIM TO FIT AT ASSEMBLY)

(7)   FRONT SPACER

I REQD

SAND ALL SIDES AFTER ASSEMBLY

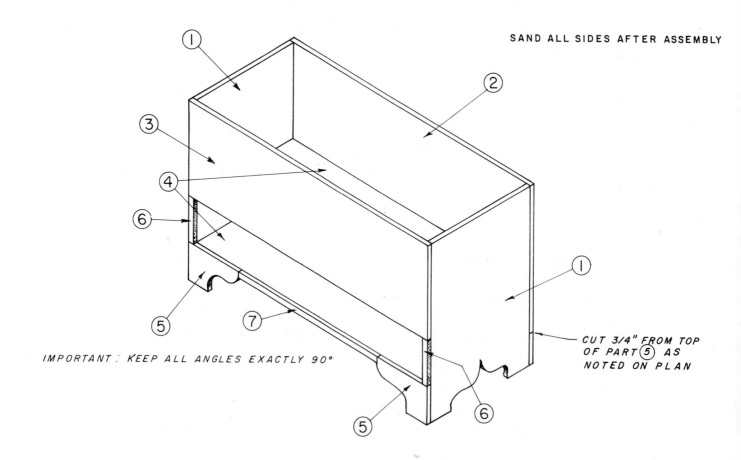

CUT 3/4" FROM TOP
OF PART (5) AS
NOTED ON PLAN

IMPORTANT : KEEP ALL ANGLES EXACTLY 90°

(8)   SUBASSEMBLY

I REQ'D

TOP VIEW

END VIEW

GLUE JOINT (AS REQ'D)

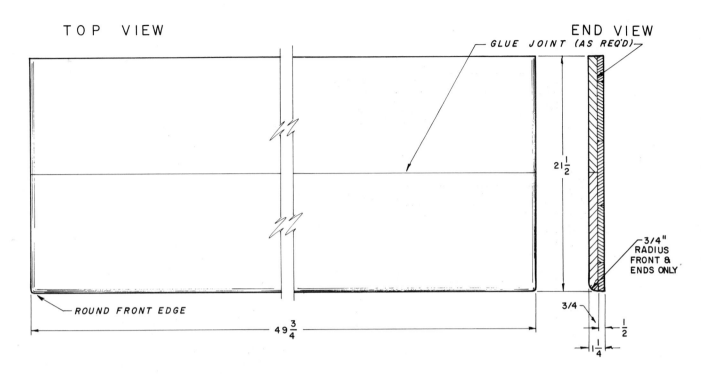

21 1/2

3/4" RADIUS FRONT & ENDS ONLY

ROUND FRONT EDGE

49 3/4

3/4

1/2

1 1/4

⑨ TOP BOARD
I REQ'D

FRONT VIEW

END VIEW

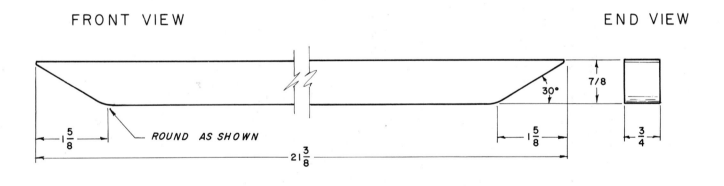

7/8

30°

ROUND AS SHOWN

1 5/8

1 5/8

3/4

21 3/8

⑩ TOP BRACE
2 REQ'D

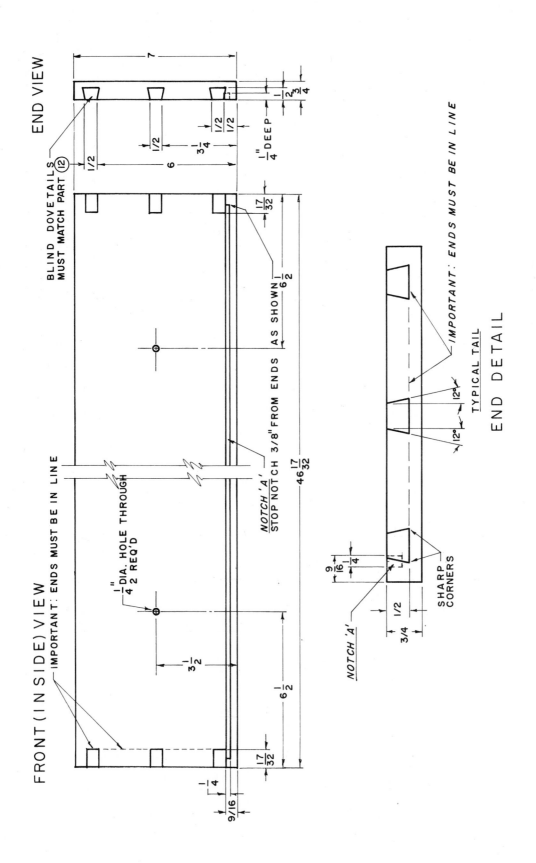

END VIEW

BLIND DOVETAILS
MUST MATCH PART (12)

7

$\frac{2}{3}$
$\frac{3}{4}$
$1\frac{2}{3}{4}$

1/2
1/2

1/2

3$\frac{1}{4}$

6

$\frac{1}{4}$" DEEP

$\frac{17}{32}$

$6\frac{1}{2}$

AS SHOWN

NOTCH 'A'
STOP NOTCH 3/8" FROM ENDS

$46\frac{17}{32}$

FRONT (INSIDE) VIEW
IMPORTANT: ENDS MUST BE IN LINE

$\frac{1}{4}$" DIA. HOLE THROUGH
2 REQ'D

$3\frac{1}{2}$

$6\frac{1}{2}$

$\frac{17}{32}$

$1\frac{1}{4}$

9/16

IMPORTANT: ENDS MUST BE IN LINE

TYPICAL TAIL

END DETAIL

12°

12°

NOTCH 'A'

$\frac{9}{16}$
$\frac{1}{4}$

1/2

3/4

SHARP
CORNERS

(11) DRAWER FRONT
1 REQ'D

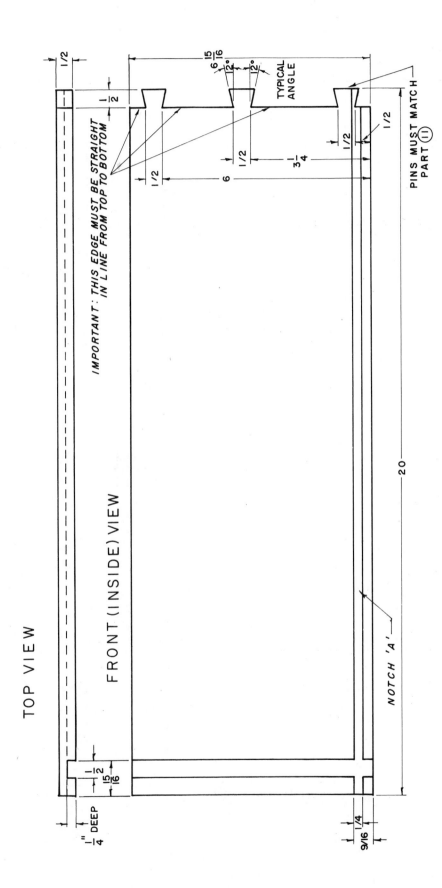

FRONT (INSIDE) VIEW

END VIEW

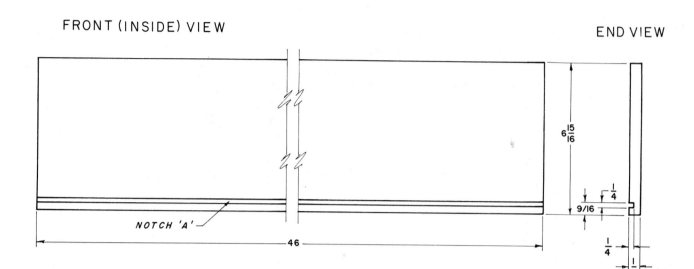

NOTCH 'A'

$6\frac{15}{16}$

$\frac{1}{4}$

9/16

46

$\frac{1}{4}$

$\frac{1}{2}$

⑬   DRAWER BACK

I REQ'D

TOP VIEW

END VIEW

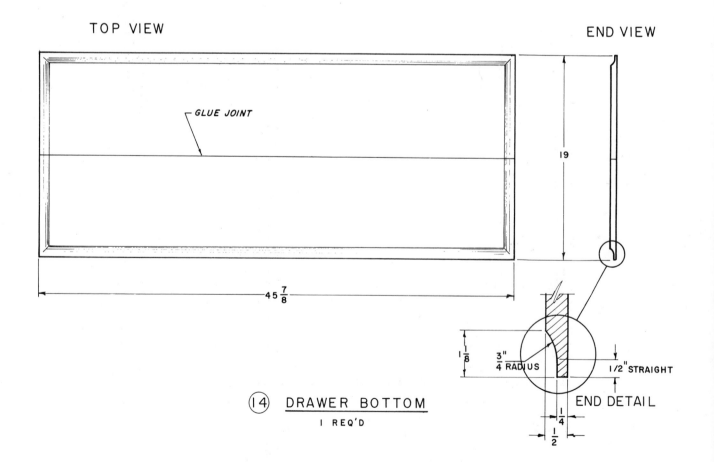

GLUE JOINT

19

$45\frac{7}{8}$

$1\frac{1}{8}$

$\frac{3}{4}$" RADIUS

$\frac{1}{4}$

$\frac{1}{2}$

$\frac{1}{2}$" STRAIGHT

END DETAIL

⑭   DRAWER BOTTOM

I REQ'D

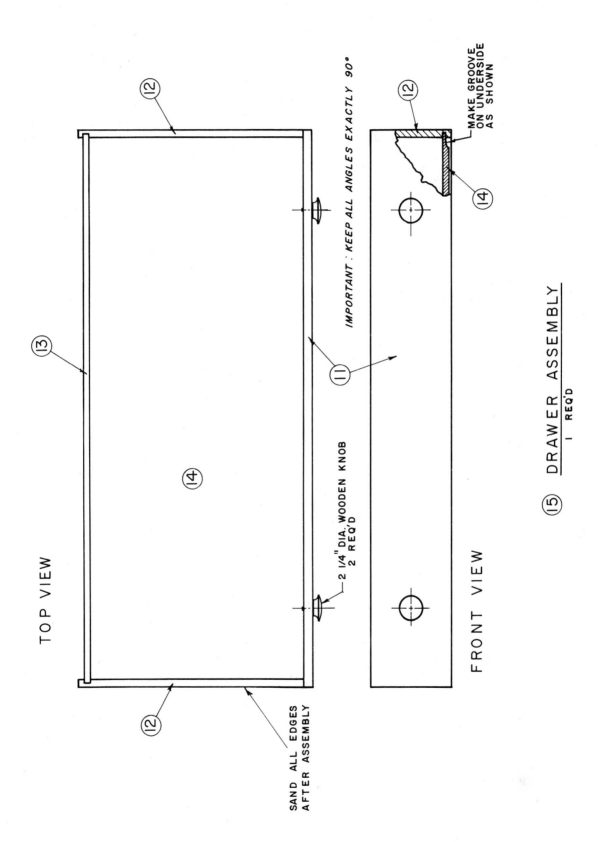

TOP VIEW

SAND ALL EDGES
AFTER ASSEMBLY

2 1/4" DIA. WOODEN KNOB
2 REQ'D

IMPORTANT : KEEP ALL ANGLES EXACTLY 90°

MAKE GROOVE
ON UNDERSIDE
AS SHOWN

FRONT VIEW

DRAWER ASSEMBLY
1 REQ'D

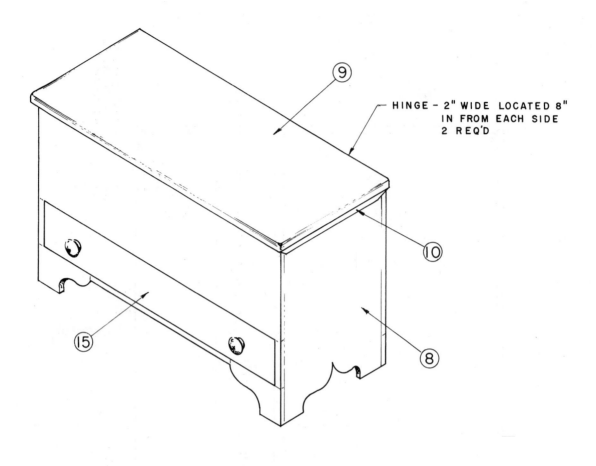

HINGE – 2" WIDE LOCATED 8"
IN FROM EACH SIDE
2 REQ'D

⑯   ASSEMBLY

Jelly Cupboard

This simple cupboard is easy to make and will add charm to any room. It is especially useful for storing all those odds and ends that you never seem to have a spot for. The proportions are especially pleasing to the eye and help to make the cupboard quite a conversation piece. This type of cupboard was in use around 1850; individual cupboards varied somewhat in height and width. Care must be taken in reproducing the ¼-inch bead and in putting together the door assembly to ensure that the bead makes a neat 90° angle.

MATERIALS

(Recommended wood: butternut, cherry, or pine)
two 1-by-12-inch 10-foot-long boards
four 1-by-6-inch 10-foot-long boards
one 1-by-2-inch 6-foot-long board
one ½-by-8-inch 4-foot-long board
one ¼-by-8-inch 4-foot-long board
one ⁵⁄₁₆-inch-diameter dowel—3 feet long
one ¾-inch-diameter wooden knob
two 2-inch-long brass hinges
thirty-six sixpenny finish nails
Water putty
Wood glue
Sandpaper—medium and fine
Stain or paint of your choice
Tung oil
Wash

INSTRUCTIONS

Cut all parts to the sizes and shapes specified in the detail drawings. The ¼-inch bead can be made with a standard Sears #9-2352 (or equivalent) molding cutter. Top and side molding (figures 7 and 8) are standard molding found in most lumber yards. If you use a hardwood for this project, you probably will have to cut your own molding in order to end up with matching wood. If the jelly cupboard is to be painted, of course, any molding will do. Assemble the main subassembly as shown in figure 10. (This part of the project is rather simple.)

Do all the necessary door beading at one setting, so it will all match. Cut the top and bottom panels, center rail, and door side panel (figures 11, 12, and 13) to match the detail drawings. Cut the ¼-inch notch for the panels (figures 14 and 15) as illustrated; cut mortises and tenons as shown. For the last step, cut the 45° angles in each part as shown. Check and recheck each step as you proceed, and compare your actual work with the detail drawings. Dry-fit each piece as it is made. Assemble the door as shown in figure 16; make it a little oversize, and fit it at assembly with the main subassembly. Add the hinges and the latch to the final assembly.

FINISH

Sand all over, distress slightly, and resand. Paint or stain to suit. Add a wash coat and allow to dry; then add a light coat of tung oil.

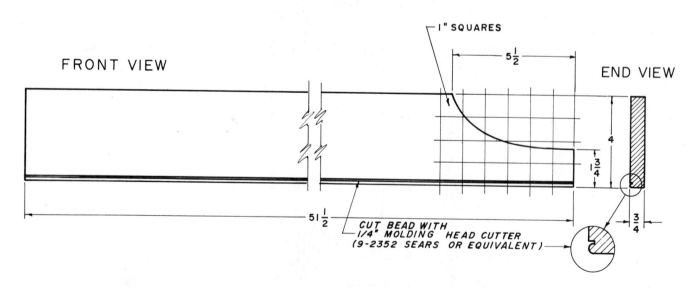

FRONT VIEW

1" SQUARES

5½

END VIEW

4

1¾

51½

CUT BEAD WITH ¼" MOLDING HEAD CUTTER (9-2352 SEARS OR EQUIVALENT)

¾

① FRONT PANEL (LEG)
1 REQ'D AS SHOWN
1 REQ'D OPPOSITE SHOWN

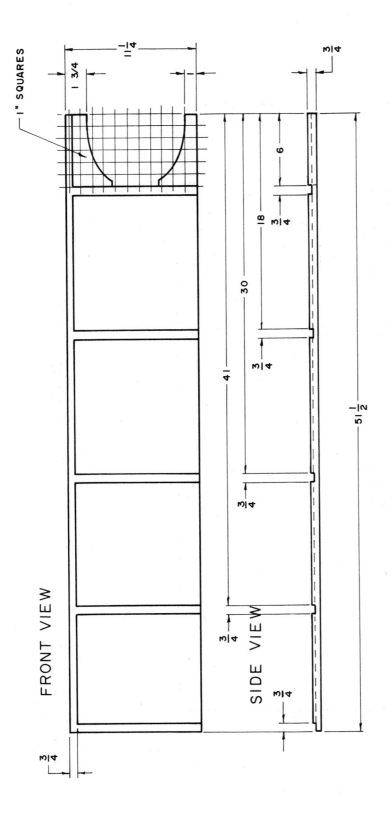

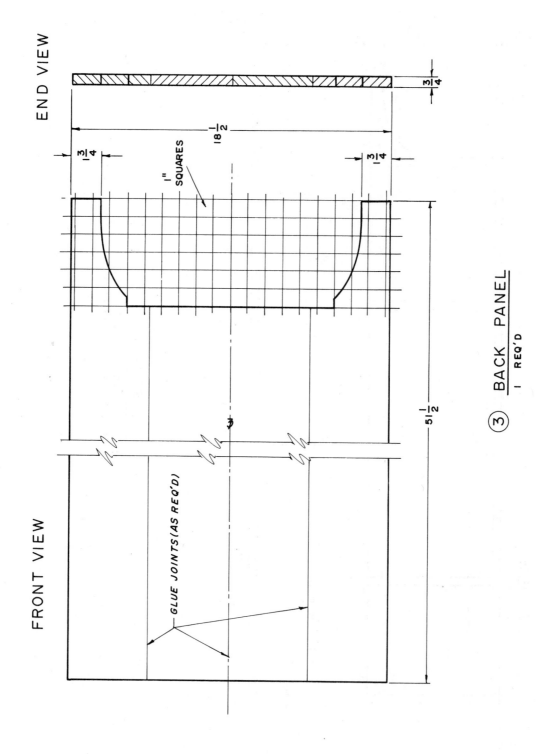

END VIEW

FRONT VIEW

GLUE JOINTS (AS REQ'D)

1" SQUARES

$18\frac{1}{2}$

$\frac{3}{4}$

$\frac{3}{4}$

$\frac{3}{4}$

$51\frac{1}{2}$

③ BACK PANEL
1 REQ'D

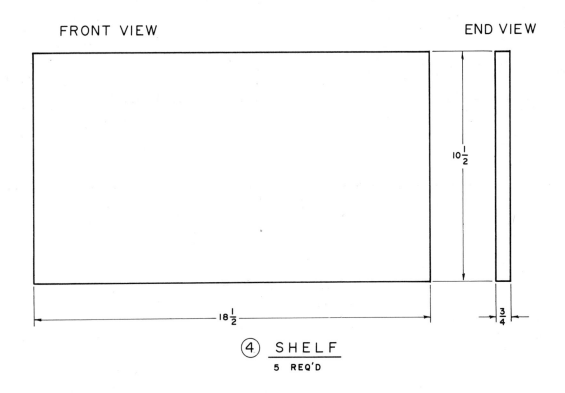

FRONT VIEW   END VIEW

$10\frac{1}{2}$

$18\frac{1}{2}$

$\frac{3}{4}$

④ S H E L F
5 REQ'D

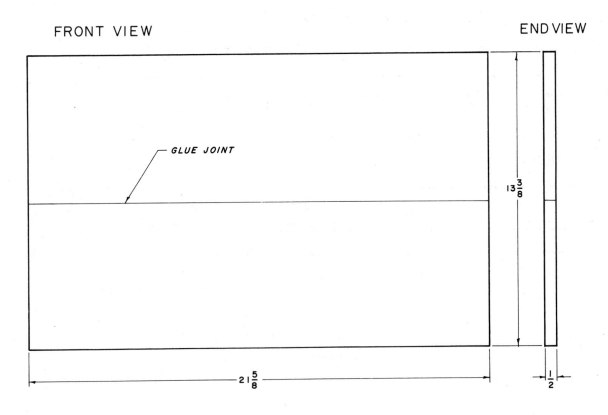

FRONT VIEW   END VIEW

GLUE JOINT

$13\frac{3}{8}$

$21\frac{5}{8}$

$\frac{1}{2}$

⑤ TOP BOARD
1 REQ'D

FRONT VIEW

END VIEW

1 $\frac{3}{4}$

11

$\frac{3}{4}$

⑥ TOP TRIM STRIP

1 REQ'D

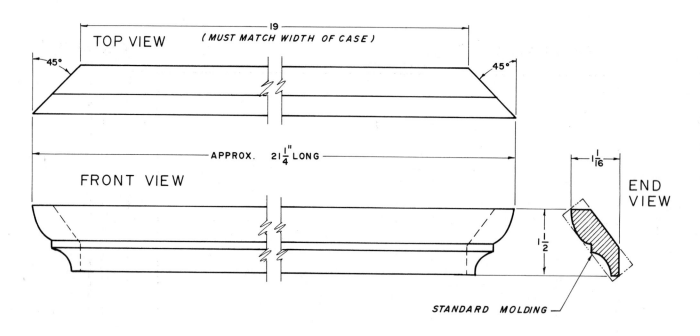

19

TOP VIEW   (MUST MATCH WIDTH OF CASE)

45°   45°

APPROX. 21 $\frac{1}{4}$" LONG

FRONT VIEW

1 $\frac{1}{16}$

END
VIEW

1 $\frac{1}{2}$

STANDARD MOLDING

⑦ FRONT MOLDING

1 REQ'D

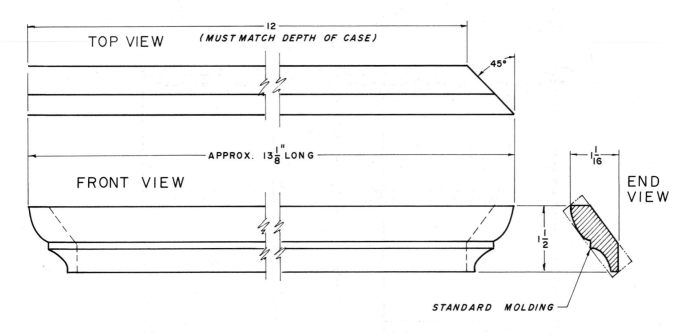

TOP VIEW (MUST MATCH DEPTH OF CASE)

12

45°

APPROX. 13⅛" LONG

FRONT VIEW

1 1/16

END VIEW

1½

STANDARD MOLDING

⑧ SIDE MOLDING

I REQ'D. AS SHOWN
I REQ'D OPPOSITE SHOWN

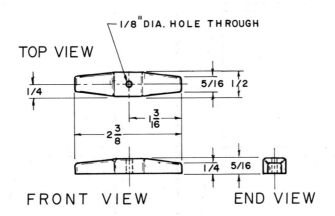

1/8" DIA. HOLE THROUGH

TOP VIEW

1/4

5/16 1/2

1 3/16

2 3/8

1/4 5/16

FRONT VIEW

END VIEW

⑨ DOOR LATCH

I REQ'D

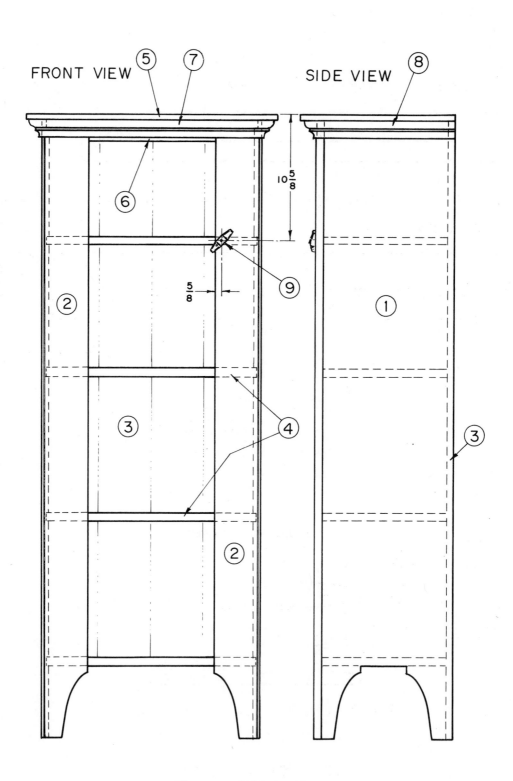

FRONT VIEW

SIDE VIEW

$10\frac{5}{8}$

$\frac{5}{8}$

⑩   SUBASSEMBLY
       1 REQ'D

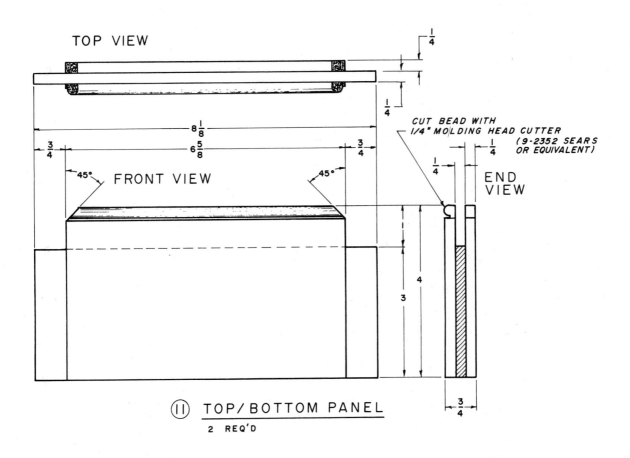

TOP VIEW

FRONT VIEW

END VIEW

$\frac{1}{4}$

$\frac{1}{4}$

CUT BEAD WITH
1/4" MOLDING HEAD CUTTER
(9-2352 SEARS
OR EQUIVALENT)

$8\frac{1}{8}$

$\frac{3}{4}$ $6\frac{5}{8}$ $\frac{3}{4}$

45°   45°

$\frac{1}{4}$ $\frac{1}{4}$

4

3

$\frac{3}{4}$

(11) TOP/BOTTOM PANEL

2 REQ'D

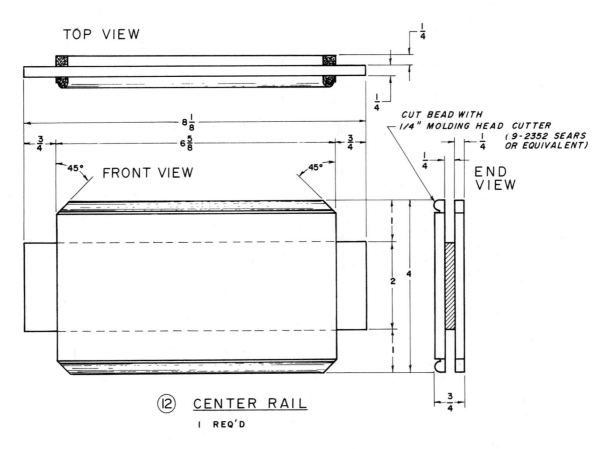

TOP VIEW

FRONT VIEW

END VIEW

$\frac{1}{4}$

$\frac{1}{4}$

CUT BEAD WITH
1/4" MOLDING HEAD CUTTER
(9-2352 SEARS
OR EQUIVALENT)

$8\frac{1}{8}$

$\frac{3}{4}$ $6\frac{5}{8}$ $\frac{3}{4}$

45°   45°

$\frac{1}{4}$ $\frac{1}{4}$

4

2

$\frac{3}{4}$

(12) CENTER RAIL

1 REQ'D

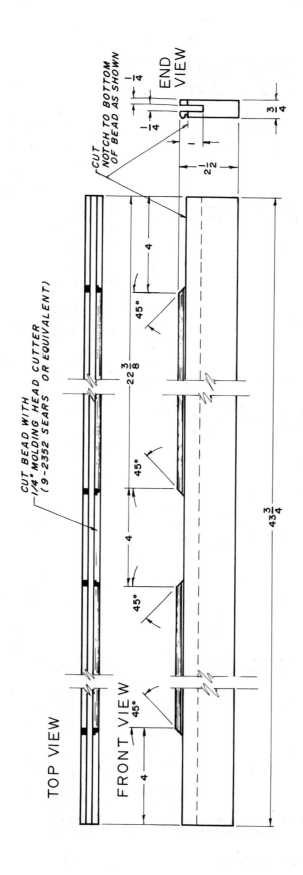

TOP VIEW

FRONT VIEW

CUT BEAD WITH
1/4" MOLDING HEAD CUTTER
(9-2352 SEARS OR EQUIVALENT)

CUT NOTCH TO BOTTOM
OF BEAD AS SHOWN

END VIEW

45°

45°

45°

45°

45°

4

4

4

4

$22\frac{3}{8}$

$43\frac{3}{4}$

$\frac{1}{4}$

$\frac{1}{4}$

$\frac{3}{4}$

$2\frac{1}{2}$

(13) SIDE PANEL (DOOR)

1 REQ'D AS SHOWN
1 REQ'D OPPOSITE SHOWN

FRONT VIEW

END VIEW

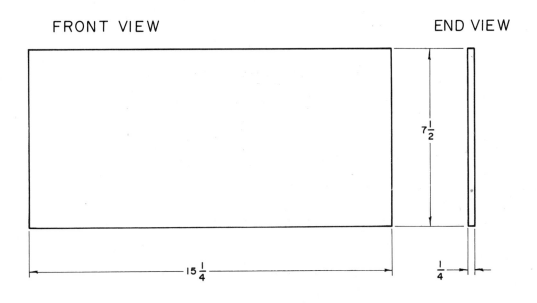

$7\frac{1}{2}$

$15\frac{1}{4}$

$\frac{1}{4}$

⑭ TOP PANEL (DOOR)

I REQ'D

FRONT VIEW

END VIEW

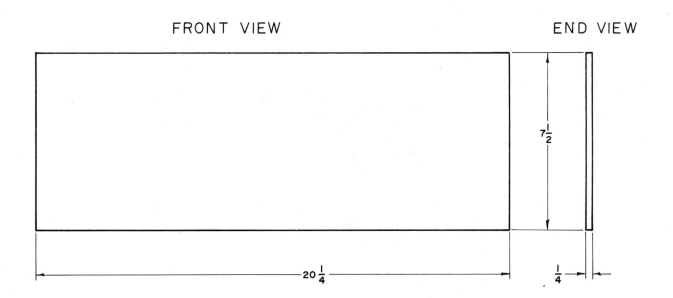

$7\frac{1}{2}$

$20\frac{1}{4}$

$\frac{1}{4}$

⑮ BOTTOM PANEL (DOOR)

I REQ'D

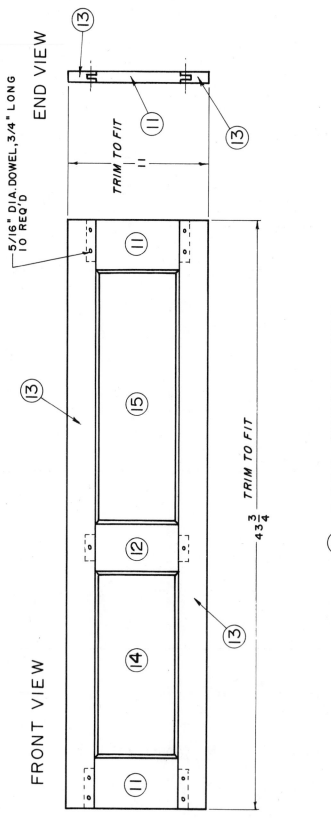

END VIEW

5/16" DIA. DOWEL, 3/4" LONG
IO REQ'D

TRIM TO FIT

FRONT VIEW

43 3/4   TRIM TO FIT

(16) DOOR SUBASSEMBLY
1 REQ'D

FRONT VIEW

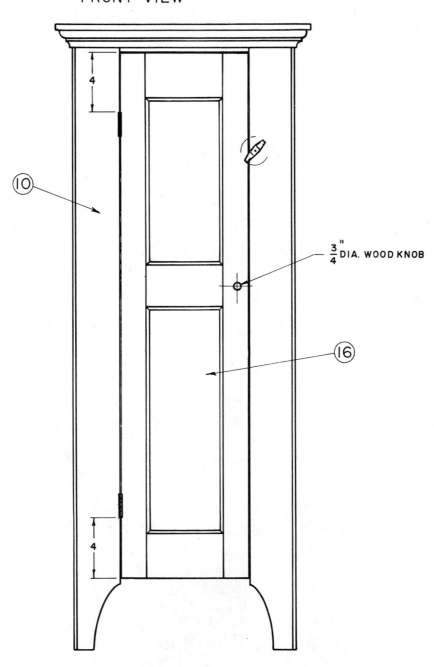

4

10

$\frac{3}{4}$" DIA. WOOD KNOB

16

4

17 ASSEMBLY

Short-Drop Schoolhouse Clock

The original "drop-octagon" schoolhouse timepiece was made by the Seth Thomas Clock Company way back in 1884. This clock is considered Victorian in style, and the Victorian influence is most evident in the octagonal wood frame. These clocks remain popular today, and the ones currently being manufactured still follow the original lines. Short-drop clocks hung not only in one-room schoolhouses but also in post offices, shops, and even saloons. After the turn of the century, barbershops came up with the idea of placing company advertisements in the center of the dial. Some even painted the numbers on the dial backwards for the convenience of the men sitting in the barber chair. The word "regulator" was sometimes added to the bottom glass to suggest a precision timepiece—although the suggestion was not always accurate. Made of cherry wood, this project adds character to any wall.

MATERIALS

(Recommended wood: cherry, oak, or walnut)
one 1-by-4-inch 6-foot-long board
one ½-by-8-inch 6-foot long board
one ¼-by-8-inch 2-foot-long board
one P103 clockworks*
one R700 dial*
one P354 wall hanger*
two P90 brass keyhole grommets*
one P125 brass bezel with glass*
one P105 door latch*
two ¾-inch-long brass hinges
one 3½-by-3½-inch glass
twenty small square-cut nails to suit
Water putty
Wood glue
Sandpaper—medium and fine
Tung oil

*Part numbers correspond to clock-part numbers of:
Merritt's Antiques Inc.
RD 2
Douglassville, Pa. 19518

INSTRUCTIONS

Cut all required molding as shown in figure 1. The next step is the most critical. Set your miter angle at exactly 22½°. (Cut eight scrap pieces of wood to check saw setting; then adjust the setting if necessary.) Cut the required eight matching pieces as shown in figure 2, and assemble them as shown in figure 3, taking care that all joints are tight and that all eight pieces, when assembled, lie flat. Cut to size the side, top, bottom, and back boards and the front plate (figures 4, 5, 6, 7, and 8). The back board (figure 8) should be glued up from scrap pine, if available. (Seth Thomas would never have wasted good wood for a back board.)

Assemble the above parts as shown in figure 9. Cut all required molding trim as shown in figure 10. Carefully cut the side, bottom, and door molding (figures 11, 12, 13, 14, and 15) from the molding trim. Take care that each pair matches exactly.

From scrap pine, cut a 5/16-by-½-inch piece of door trim, 18 inches long. From this scrap piece, cut the door top, bottom, and side pieces (figures 16, 17, and 18). Assemble these with the shims as shown in figure 19. Fill and sand all edges and corners. Make the door subassembly as shown in figure 21; cut the door glass (figure 20), and insert it into the subassembly. Sand all over and attach the door to the completed case assembly (figure 22). Add the door latch and hanger. It is necessary to add a 1/16-inch-thick spacer or shim as indicated on the door subassembly diagram (figure 21) to allow the door to swing flush when closed.

FINISH

Fill and sand all over. Give the case three or four coats of tung oil, sanding lightly between coats. Fit in the clockworks, taking care that the center of the hand shaft is in the exact center of the main ring (shim if necessary). Add the pendulum and hang the clock level on the wall; then wind and adjust the works.

Temporarily add the hands, and run the clock for two or three days. If everything runs correctly, fit the dial, the brass bezel with glass, and the hands. If necessary, carefully locate and drill holes for the key winds. Add the brass keyhole grommets. Adjust the pendulum so the clock keeps exact time (up to speed up the clock; down to slow down the clock).

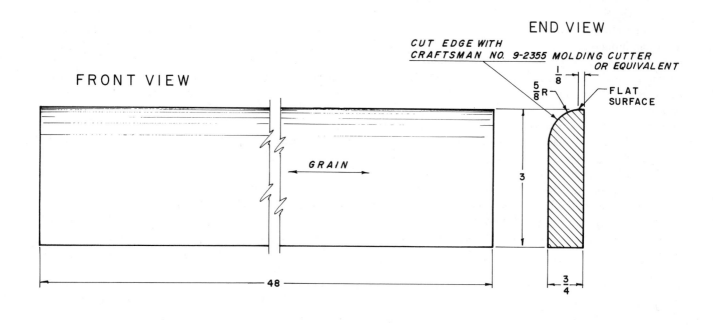

END VIEW

CUT EDGE WITH
CRAFTSMAN NO. 9-2355 MOLDING CUTTER
OR EQUIVALENT

FRONT VIEW

$\frac{1}{8}$

$\frac{5}{8}$R

FLAT
SURFACE

3

GRAIN

48

$\frac{3}{4}$

① MOLDING
1 REQ'D

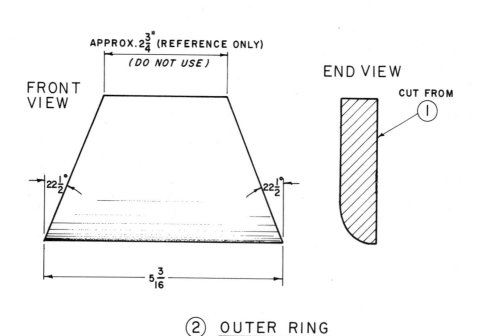

APPROX. $2\frac{3}{4}$" (REFERENCE ONLY)

(DO NOT USE)

FRONT
VIEW

END VIEW

CUT FROM

①

$22\frac{1}{2}°$ $22\frac{1}{2}°$

$5\frac{3}{16}$

② OUTER RING
8 REQ'D

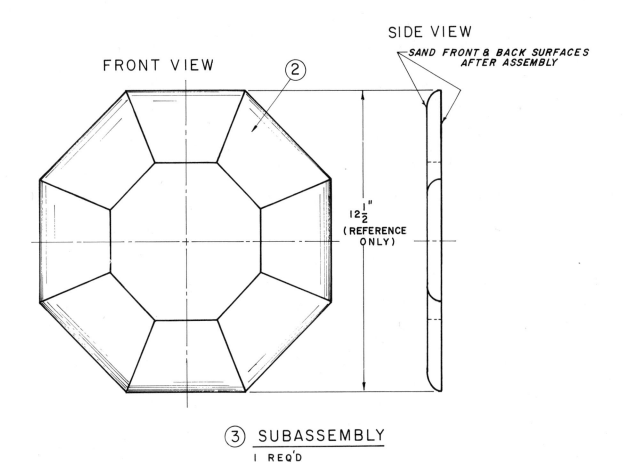

FRONT VIEW

SIDE VIEW

SAND FRONT & BACK SURFACES
AFTER ASSEMBLY

12 1/2"
(REFERENCE
ONLY)

③ SUBASSEMBLY
1 REQ'D

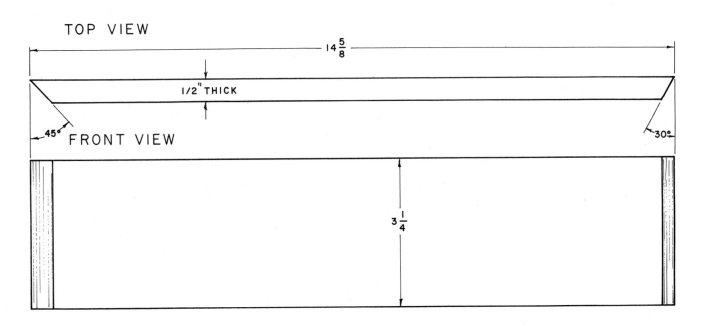

TOP VIEW

14 5/8

1/2" THICK

45°

FRONT VIEW

30°

3 1/4

④ SIDE BOARD
2 REQ'D

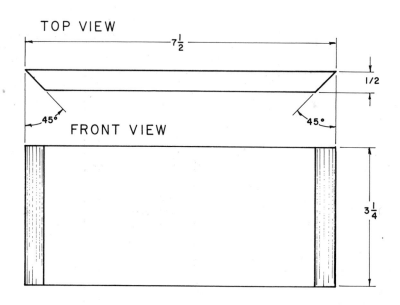

(5) TOP BOARD
1 REQ'D

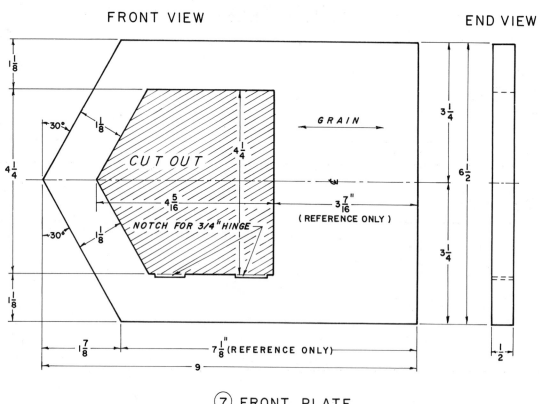

(7) FRONT PLATE
1 REQ'D

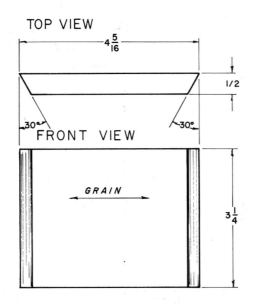

TOP VIEW

$4\frac{5}{16}$

$1/2$

30° 30°

FRONT VIEW

GRAIN

$3\frac{1}{4}$

⑥ BOTTOM BOARD
2 REQ'D

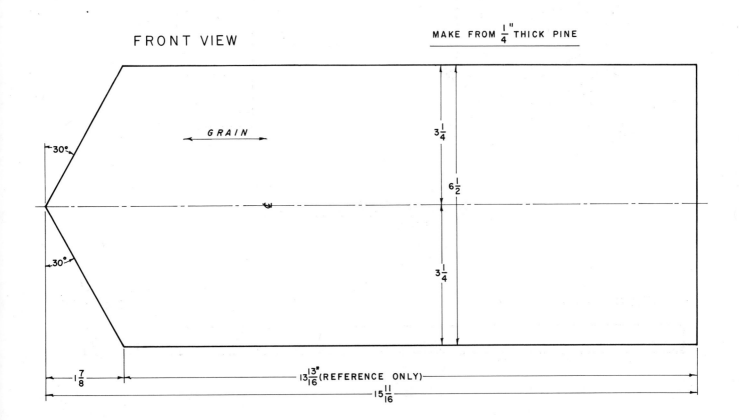

FRONT VIEW

MAKE FROM $\frac{1}{4}$" THICK PINE

GRAIN

30°

30°

$3\frac{1}{4}$

$6\frac{1}{2}$

$3\frac{1}{4}$

$1\frac{7}{8}$

$13\frac{13}{16}$" (REFERENCE ONLY)

$15\frac{11}{16}$

⑧ BACK BOARD
1 REQ'D

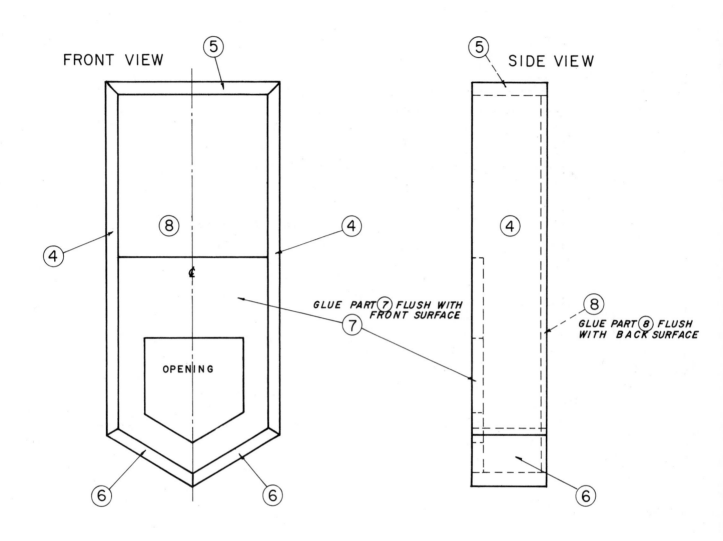

FRONT VIEW

SIDE VIEW

GLUE PART ⑦ FLUSH WITH
FRONT SURFACE

GLUE PART ⑧ FLUSH
WITH BACK SURFACE

OPENING

⑨ BODY SUBASSEMBLY
I REQ'D

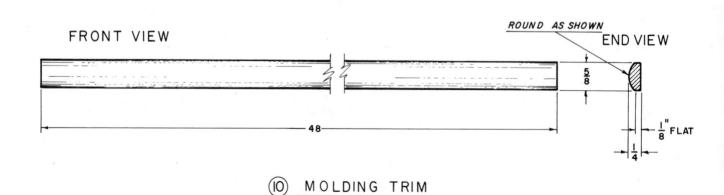

ROUND AS SHOWN

FRONT VIEW

END VIEW

$\frac{5}{8}$

$\frac{1}{8}$" FLAT

$\frac{1}{4}$

48

⑩ MOLDING TRIM
I REQ'D

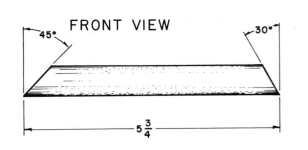

FRONT VIEW

45° 30°

5 3/4

CUT FROM PART ⑩

END VIEW

⑩

⑪ SIDE MOLDING
I REQ'D AS SHOWN
I REQ'D OPPOSITE SHOWN

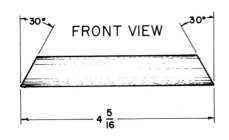

30° FRONT VIEW 30°

4 5/16

CUT FROM PART ⑩

END VIEW ⑩

⑫ BOTTOM MOLDING
2 REQ'D

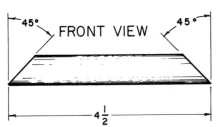

45° FRONT VIEW 45°

4 1/2

CUT FROM PART ⑩

END VIEW

⑩

⑬ DOOR MOLDING (TOP)
I REQ'D

FRONT VIEW

30° 45°

3 1/4

CUT FROM PART ⑩

END VIEW

⑩

⑭ DOOR MOLDING (SIDE)
I REQ'D AS SHOWN
I REQ'D OPPOSITE SHOWN

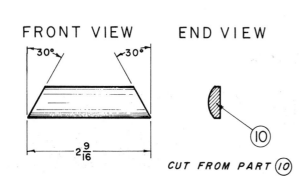

FRONT VIEW   END VIEW

30°   30°

2 9/16

CUT FROM PART ⑩

⑮ DOOR MOLDING (BOTTOM)
2 REQ'D

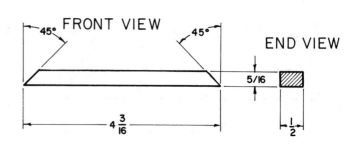

FRONT VIEW   END VIEW

45°   45°

4 3/16

5/16

1/2

⑯ DOOR TOP
I REQ'D

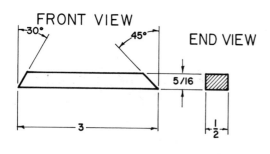

FRONT VIEW   END VIEW

30°   45°

5/16

3

1/2

⑰ DOOR SIDE
2 REQ'D

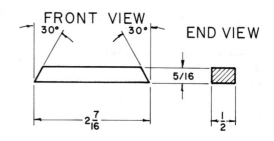

FRONT VIEW   END VIEW

30°   30°

5/16

2 7/16

1/2

⑱ DOOR BOTTOM
2 REQ'D

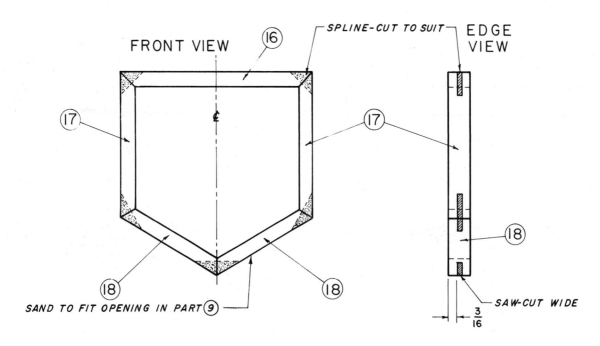

SPLINE-CUT TO SUIT   EDGE VIEW

FRONT VIEW   ⑯

⑰   ⑰

⑱   ⑱

SAND TO FIT OPENING IN PART ⑨

SAW-CUT WIDE

3/16

⑲ SUBASSEMBLY
I REQ'D

FRONT VIEW

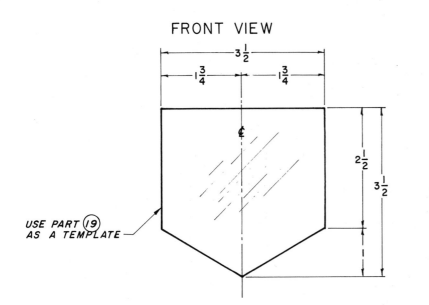

USE PART ⑲
AS A TEMPLATE

㉠ DOOR GLASS
⎯⎯⎯⎯⎯⎯⎯⎯
I REQ'D

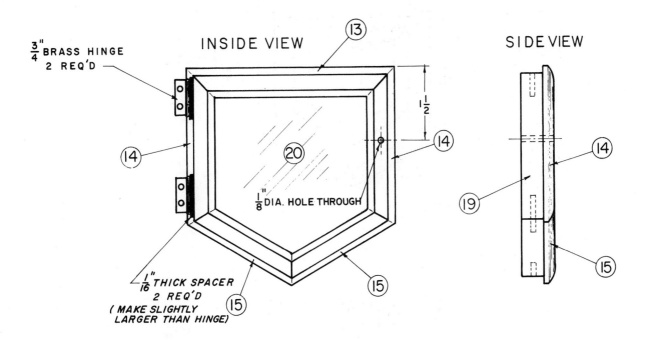

INSIDE VIEW

SIDE VIEW

㉑ SUBASSEMBLY
⎯⎯⎯⎯⎯⎯⎯⎯⎯
I REQ'D

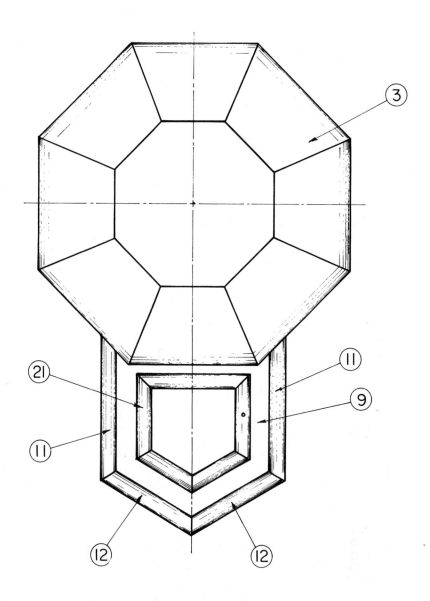

22 SUBASSEMBLY
I REQ'D

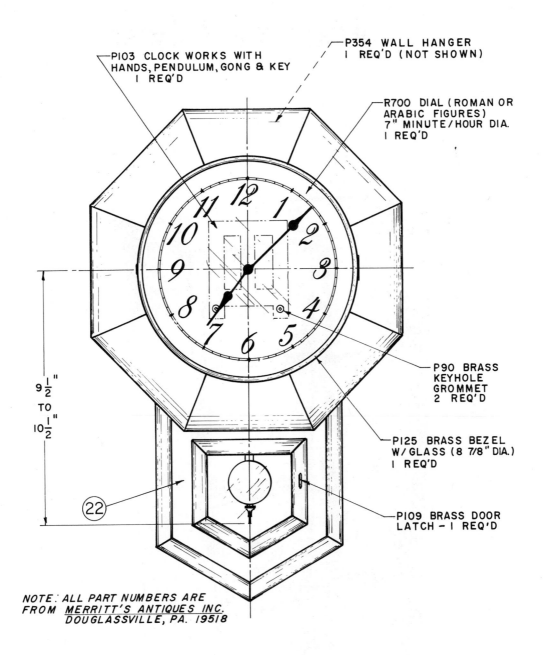

P103 CLOCK WORKS WITH
HANDS, PENDULUM, GONG & KEY
1 REQ'D

P354 WALL HANGER
1 REQ'D (NOT SHOWN)

R700 DIAL (ROMAN OR
ARABIC FIGURES)
7" MINUTE/HOUR DIA.
1 REQ'D

P90 BRASS
KEYHOLE
GROMMET
2 REQ'D

P125 BRASS BEZEL
W/GLASS (8 7/8" DIA.)
1 REQ'D

P109 BRASS DOOR
LATCH - 1 REQ'D

9 1/2"
TO
10 1/2"

(22)

NOTE: ALL PART NUMBERS ARE
FROM *MERRITT'S ANTIQUES INC.*
DOUGLASSVILLE, PA. 19518

(23) <u>ASSEMBLY</u>
1 REQ'D

Apothecary Chest

The apothecary chest was an important accessory for the pharmacist of yesterday. Similar chests were used by the undertaker, the barber, the dentist, the storekeeper, the blacksmith, and the dry goods merchant. This chest will still prove to be very useful today: it makes a great storage area for most anything and everything. Its nicest feature is that is does not take up much floor space in relation to its storage capacity. Most antique apothecary chests were made either of oak or of pine (as was the original of this project). This is a fun project if you like a lot of repetitious work. The ten drawers should be exactly the same size, so that they will be interchangeable. This requires a lot of care. Don't be alarmed if, at times, the drawers are too long. They will expand and contract by as much as ³⁄₁₆ of an inch from spring to winter.

MATERIALS

(Recommended wood: walnut or pine)
two 1-by-12-inch 10-foot-long boards
one 1-by-8-inch 10-foot-long board
two ½-by-8-inch 12-foot-long boards
one ⅜-by-8-inch 8-foot-long board
one ³⁄₁₆-by-8-inch 8-foot-long board
thirty-six square-cut nails to suit
ten ¾-inch-diameter white milk-glass knobs
Water putty
Wood glue
Sandpaper—medium and fine
Stain of your choice
Tung oil
Wash
#0000 steel wool

INSTRUCTIONS

Although rather small, this apothecary chest requires a lot of wood to make. It is extremely important that all dimensions be followed very closely, that all notches be cut at exactly 90° from front to back, and that pairs of the same part match exactly. It is a good idea for all cuts to be made using the same saw adjustments and for "stops" or jigs to be used to ensure identical parts.

Cut to size the parts shown in figures 1 through 6 and in figure 12. Assemble these parts as shown in figure 13. Be sure all surfaces are square and fit tightly. Cut to size the drawer parts (figures 7 through 10), and assemble each drawer as shown in figure 11. Sand each drawer after assembly. All drawers should be exactly the same size and should be interchangeable. If the pigeonholes for the drawers are not exactly the same size, each drawer will have to be fit and numbered individually to ensure a good fit for each.

FINISH

Sand all over, distress lightly, and resand. Stain to suit and apply two coats of tung oil, a wash coat, and a final coat of tung oil. Add the ten white milk-glass drawer knobs.

SIDE VIEW

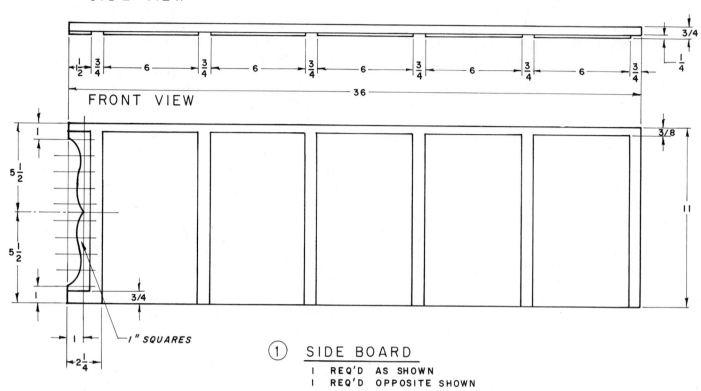

① SIDE BOARD
1 REQ'D AS SHOWN
1 REQ'D OPPOSITE SHOWN

SIDE VIEW

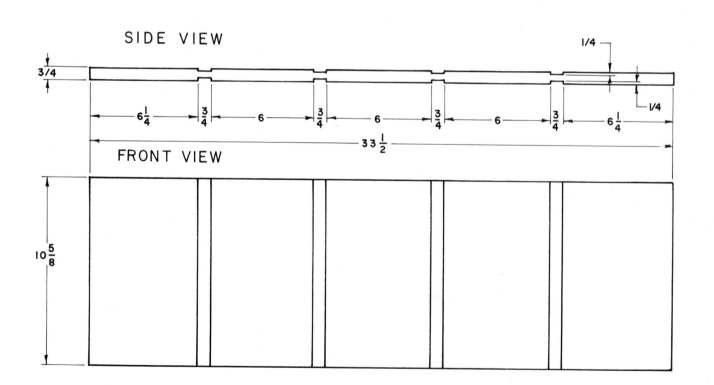

② CENTER DIVIDER
1 REQ'D

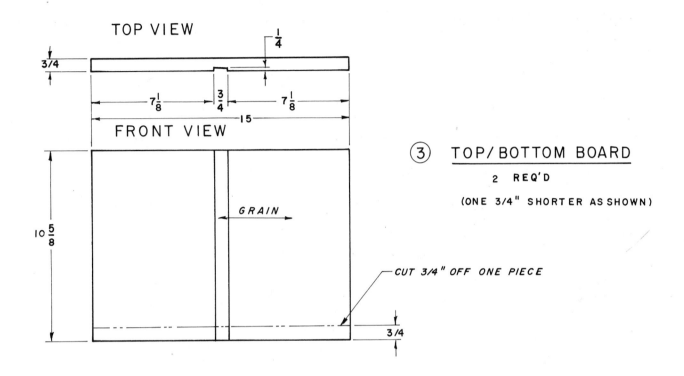

TOP VIEW

3/4

1/4

7 1/8   3/4   7 1/8

15

FRONT VIEW

GRAIN

10 5/8

(3) TOP/BOTTOM BOARD

2 REQ'D

(ONE 3/4" SHORTER AS SHOWN)

CUT 3/4" OFF ONE PIECE

3/4

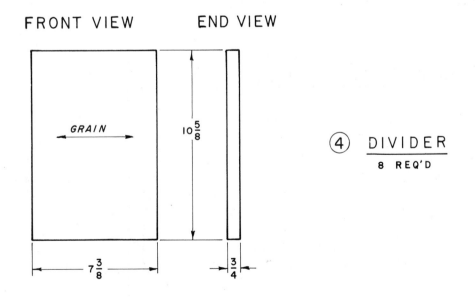

FRONT VIEW   END VIEW

GRAIN

10 5/8

7 3/8   3/4

(4) DIVIDER

8 REQ'D

TOP VIEW

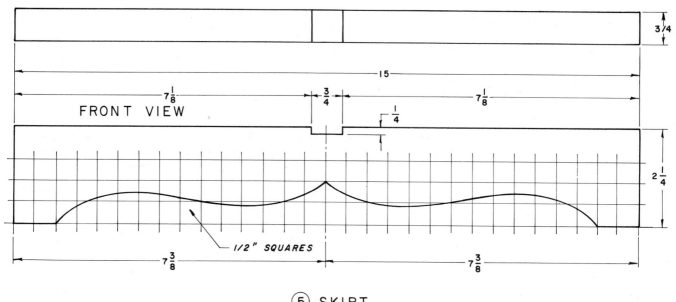

FRONT VIEW

1/2" SQUARES

⑤ SKIRT
1 REQ'D

TOP VIEW

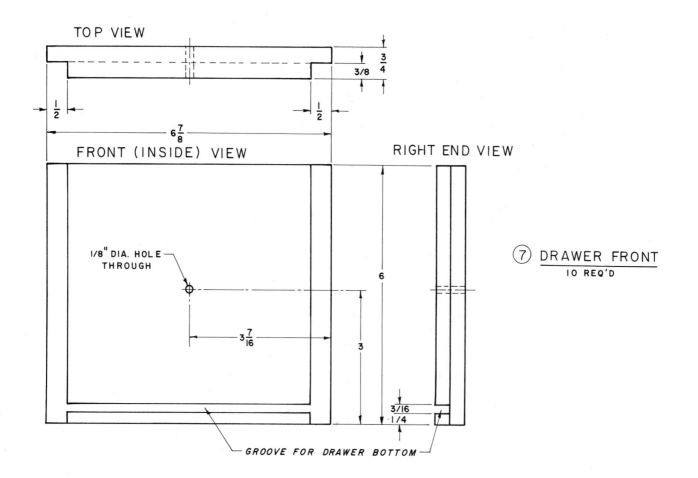

FRONT (INSIDE) VIEW

RIGHT END VIEW

1/8" DIA. HOLE
THROUGH

⑦ DRAWER FRONT
10 REQ'D

GROOVE FOR DRAWER BOTTOM

TOP VIEW

RIGHT SIDE VIEW

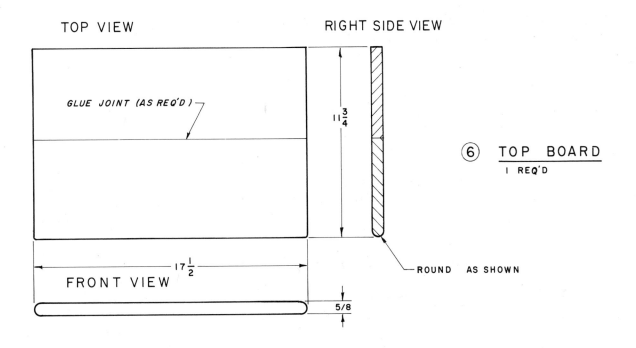

GLUE JOINT (AS REQ'D)

$11\frac{3}{4}$

⑥ TOP BOARD
1 REQ'D

ROUND AS SHOWN

$17\frac{1}{2}$

FRONT VIEW

5/8

TOP VIEW

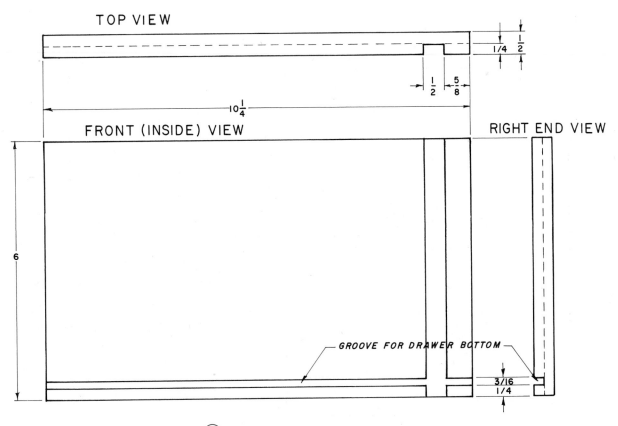

1/4 $\frac{1}{2}$

$\frac{1}{2}$ $\frac{5}{8}$

$10\frac{1}{4}$

FRONT (INSIDE) VIEW

RIGHT END VIEW

6

GROOVE FOR DRAWER BOTTOM

3/16
1/4

⑧ DRAWER SIDE
10 REQ'D AS SHOWN
10 REQ'D OPPOSITE SHOWN

FRONT VIEW (INSIDE)

RIGHT END VIEW

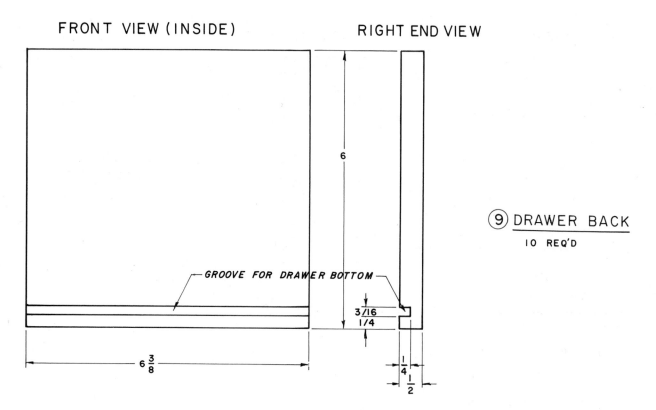

GROOVE FOR DRAWER BOTTOM

6

3/16
1/4

$6\frac{3}{8}$

$\frac{1}{4}$
$\frac{1}{2}$

⑨ DRAWER BACK

10 REQ'D

FRONT VIEW

END VIEW

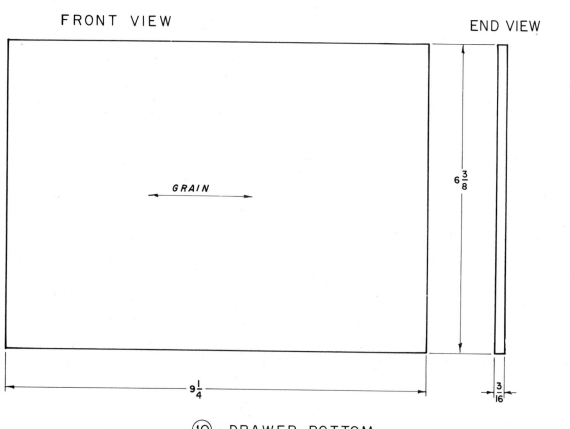

GRAIN

$6\frac{3}{8}$

$9\frac{1}{4}$

$\frac{3}{16}$

⑩   DRAWER BOTTOM

10 REQ'D

TOP VIEW

SIDE VIEW

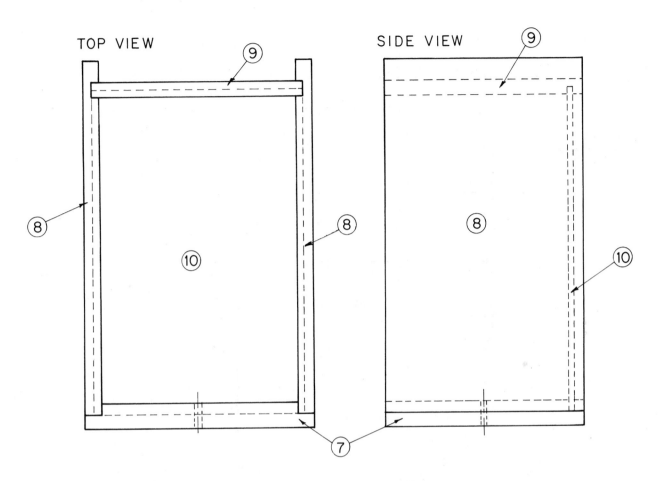

⑪ <u>SUBASSEMBLY</u>
10 REQ'D

SIDE VIEW

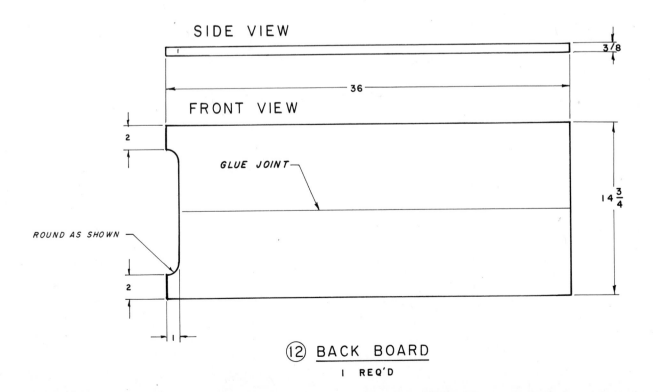

3/8

36

FRONT VIEW

2

GLUE JOINT

14 3/4

ROUND AS SHOWN

2

1

⑫ <u>BACK BOARD</u>
1 REQ'D

FRONT VIEW   SIDE VIEW

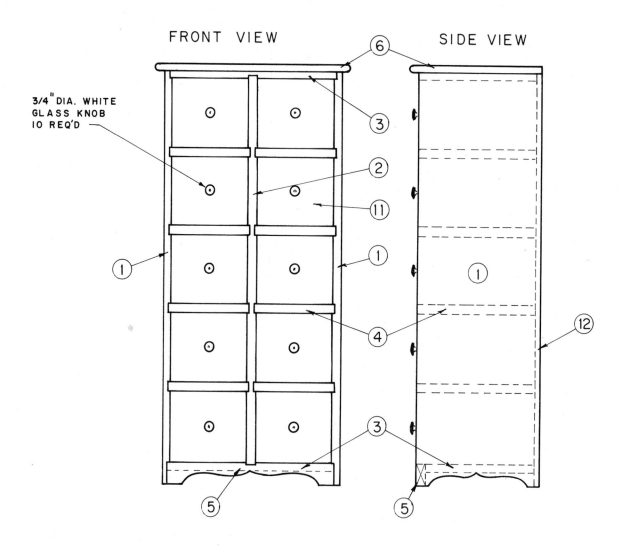

3/4" DIA. WHITE
GLASS KNOB
10 REQ'D

⑬ ASSEMBLY

Pewter Hutch

Furniture of this type became a necessity as pewter and pottery began to replace wooden plates in the homes of yesterday. At first, rails were used to hold the plates vertical, but later grooves replaced rails. These cupboards had two or three open shelves at the top for displaying pewter and a closed cupboard underneath with one or two shelves. This particular hutch is extremely thick at the base—almost disproportionately so, in fact—but this is the exact size of the original. The sides of the original were made from a single wide pine board, about 19 inches in width. Pewter cupboards gave way to the more formal china cabinets of the 1800s as low-priced pressed glass replaced pewter and pottery.

MATERIALS

(Recommended wood: pumpkin pine)
two 1-by-4-inch 8-foot-long boards
two 1-by-8-inch 10-foot-long boards
seven 1-by-12-inch 10-foot-long boards
one ½-by-10-inch 4-foot-long boards
one ⅞-by-¾-inch molding—5 feet long
one 1¾-inch-diameter wooden knob
two 2½-inch-long brass hinges
one ¼-inch-diameter dowel—3 feet long
thirty square-cut nails (very old, if possible)
one #10 round head wood screw—1½ inches long
Wood putty
Wood glue
Sandpaper—medium and fine
Stain of your choice
Wash
Tung oil
Lemon oil

INSTRUCTIONS

Glue up material for the sides (figure 1). Make a cardboard pattern of the scallop design and transfer it to the wooden material. Glue up and cut to size the parts shown in figures 2 through 8, and check that all cuts are exactly square. Using large, square-cut nails, assemble these parts. The original had the square-cut nails countersunk and filled with water putty. Do not try to stain or hide the wood putty; the original piece had white putty showing through the stain, and copying this will make your project look more authentic. Cut to size the parts shown in figures 10 through 18. Standard moldings similar to those shown in figures 11, 12, 14 and 15 can be purchased at the lumberyard, in the event that you do not have a shaper for making your own. Assemble the main subassembly as shown in figure 15, and sand it all over.

Cut to size the door parts (figures 20, 21, and 22). Sand and stain the door panel (figure 22) before assembling. Assemble the door as shown in figure 23, but do not glue the door panel (figure 22) in place—let it float freely. The eight ¼-inch-diameter dowel holes and pins can be drilled and inserted after the glue dries. Just be sure the door assembly lies absolutely flat.

Cut the door lock (figure 24) to approximate size, and attach it with the round head wood screw. Add the wooden knob as shown in figure 25. Fit and attach the door assembly.

FINISH

Sand all over, distress, and resand. Apply stain and two coats of tung oil. Add the wash coat, let dry, and apply a final coat of tung oil. Rub down with #0000 steel wool, and apply lemon oil.

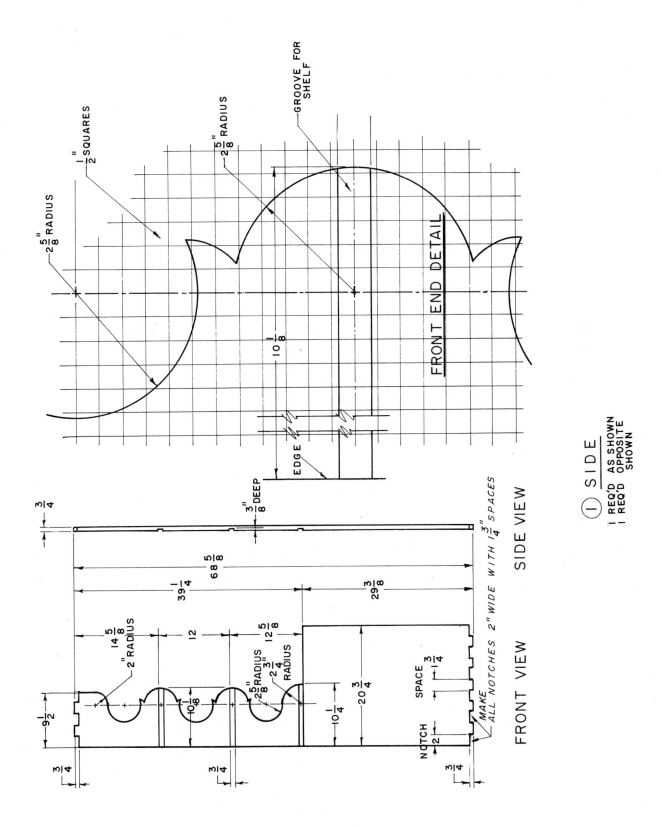

GROOVE FOR SHELF

$\frac{1}{2}$ SQUARES

$2\frac{5}{8}$" RADIUS

$2\frac{5}{8}$" RADIUS

$10\frac{1}{8}$

EDGE

FRONT END DETAIL

$\frac{3}{8}$" DEEP

$\frac{3}{4}$

$68\frac{5}{8}$

$39\frac{1}{4}$

$29\frac{3}{8}$

SIDE VIEW

$14\frac{5}{8}$

2" RADIUS

12

$12\frac{5}{8}$

$2\frac{5}{8}$" RADIUS

$2\frac{3}{4}$" RADIUS

$10\frac{1}{8}$

$10\frac{1}{4}$

$20\frac{3}{4}$

SPACE

$\frac{3}{4}$

$9\frac{1}{2}$

NOTCH

2

$\frac{3}{4}$

$\frac{3}{4}$

$\frac{3}{4}$

MAKE ALL NOTCHES 2" WIDE WITH $1\frac{3}{4}$" SPACES

FRONT VIEW

SIDE

1 REQ'D AS SHOWN
1 REQ'D OPPOSITE SHOWN

FRONT VIEW

END VIEW

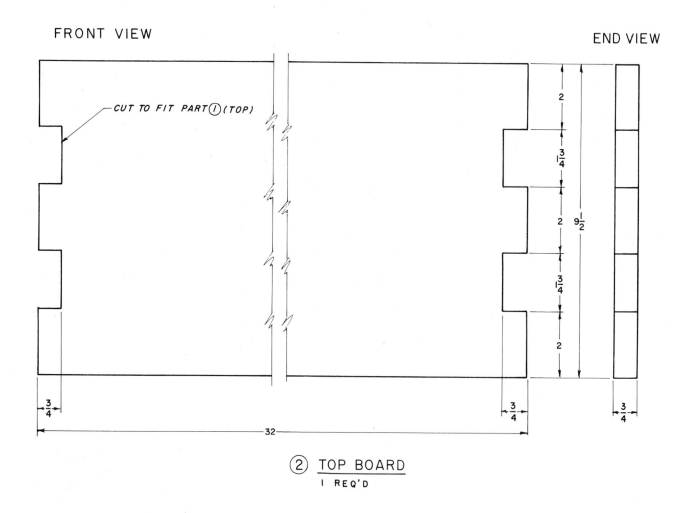

CUT TO FIT PART ① (TOP)

2

$1\frac{3}{4}$

2

$1\frac{3}{4}$

2

$9\frac{1}{2}$

$\frac{3}{4}$

$\frac{3}{4}$

$\frac{3}{4}$

32

② TOP BOARD

1 REQ'D

FRONT VIEW

END VIEW

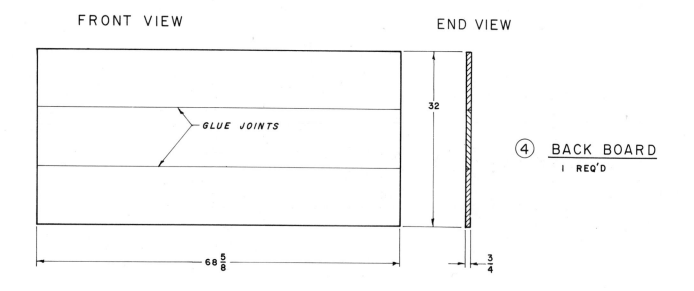

GLUE JOINTS

32

④ BACK BOARD

1 REQ'D

$68\frac{5}{8}$

$\frac{3}{4}$

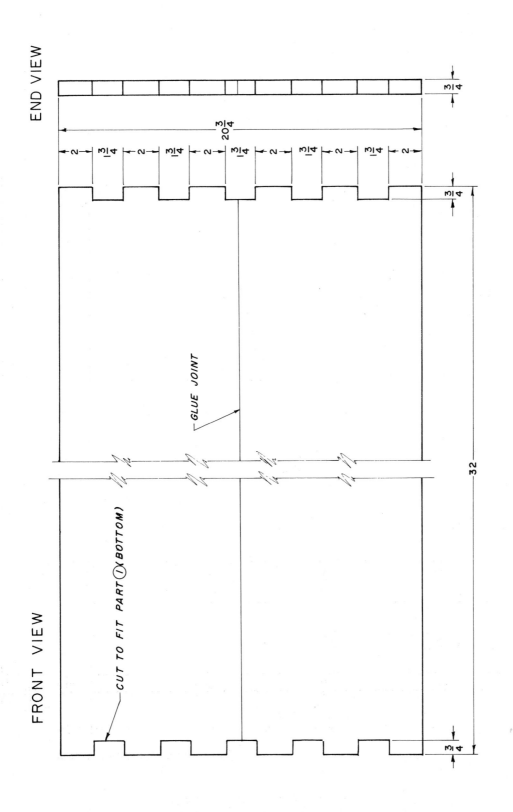

END VIEW

$20\frac{3}{4}$

$\frac{3}{4}$

2 $1\frac{3}{4}$ 2 $1\frac{3}{4}$ 2 $1\frac{3}{4}$ 2 $1\frac{3}{4}$ 2 $1\frac{3}{4}$ 2

$\frac{3}{4}$

GLUE JOINT

32

CUT TO FIT PART ① (BOTTOM)

FRONT VIEW

$\frac{3}{4}$

③ BOTTOM BOARD
I REQ'D

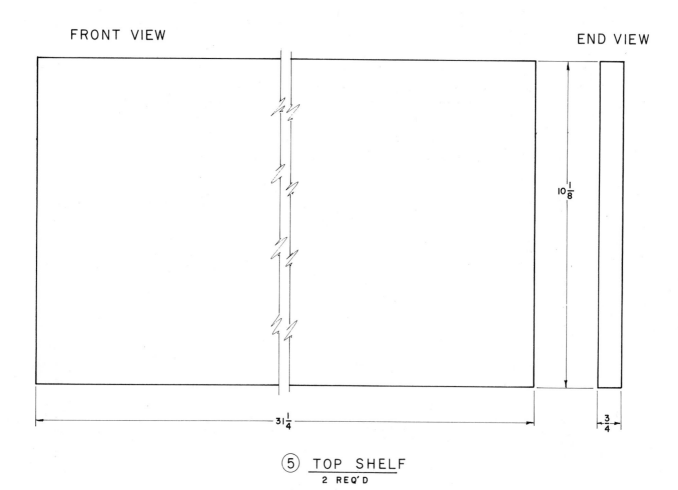

FRONT VIEW   END VIEW

$10\frac{1}{8}$

$31\frac{1}{4}$

$\frac{3}{4}$

⑤ TOP SHELF
2 REQ'D

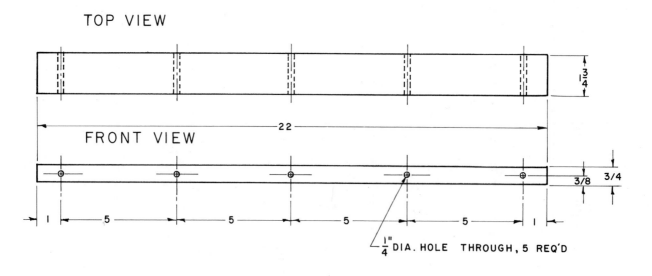

TOP VIEW

$1\frac{3}{4}$

FRONT VIEW

22

$\frac{3}{8}$ $\frac{3}{4}$

1   5   5   5   5   1

$\frac{1}{4}$" DIA. HOLE THROUGH, 5 REQ'D

⑧   SHELF END (CENTER)
2 REQ'D

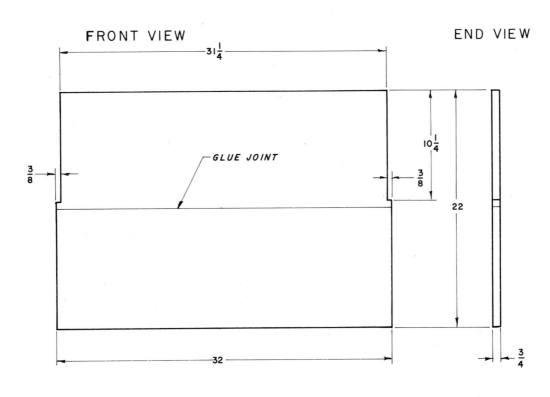

FRONT VIEW   END VIEW

$31\frac{1}{4}$

GLUE JOINT

$\frac{3}{8}$

$10\frac{1}{4}$

$\frac{3}{8}$

22

32

$\frac{3}{4}$

⑦   CENTER SHELF

1 REQ'D

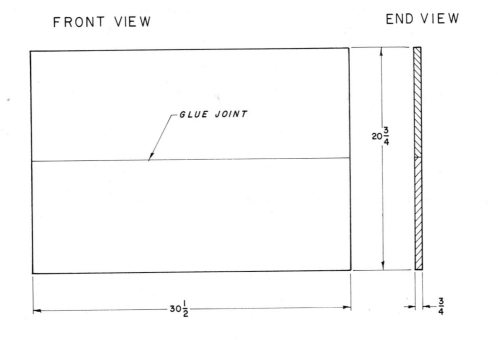

FRONT VIEW   END VIEW

GLUE JOINT

$20\frac{3}{4}$

$30\frac{1}{2}$

$\frac{3}{4}$

⑥   BOTTOM SHELF

1 REQ'D

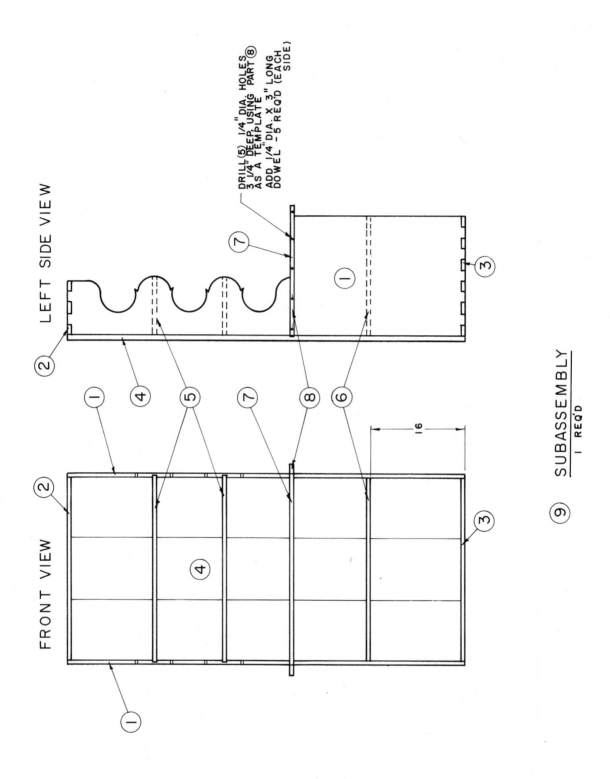

LEFT SIDE VIEW

DRILL (5) 1/4" DIA. HOLES
3 1/4" DEEP, USING PART (8)
AS A TEMPLATE
ADD 1/4" DIA. X 3" LONG
DOWEL - 5 REQ'D (EACH SIDE)

FRONT VIEW

16

SUBASSEMBLY
1 REQ'D

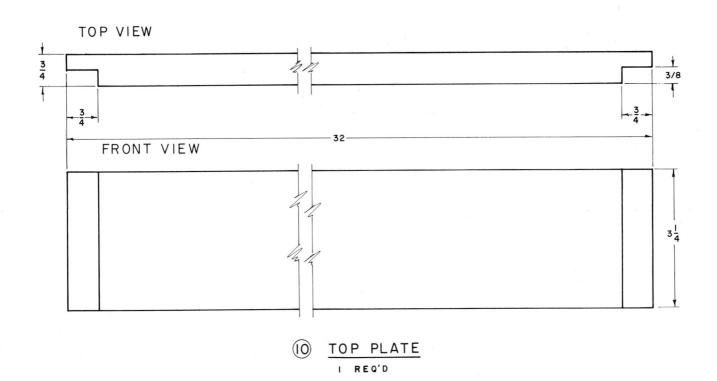

TOP VIEW

FRONT VIEW

$\frac{3}{4}$

3/8

$\frac{3}{4}$

$\frac{3}{4}$

32

$3\frac{1}{4}$

⑩ TOP PLATE

I REQ'D

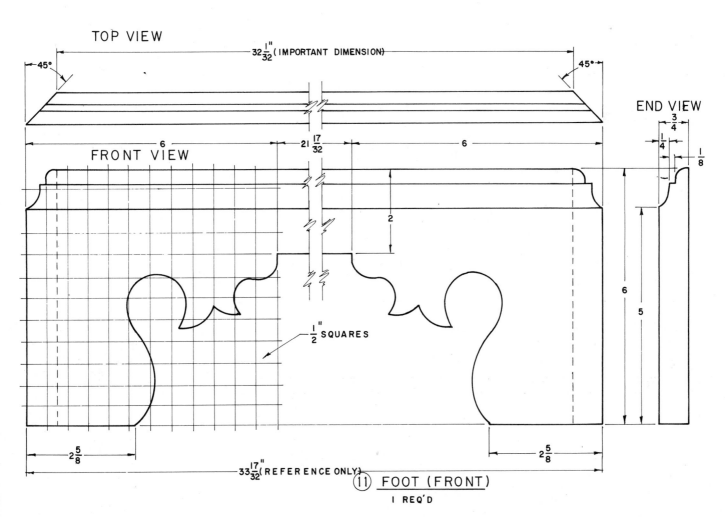

TOP VIEW

$32\frac{1}{32}$" (IMPORTANT DIMENSION)

45°

45°

END VIEW

$\frac{3}{4}$

$\frac{1}{4}$

$\frac{1}{8}$

6

$21\frac{17}{32}$

6

FRONT VIEW

2

6

5

$\frac{1}{2}$" SQUARES

$2\frac{5}{8}$

$2\frac{5}{8}$

$33\frac{17}{32}$" (REFERENCE ONLY)

⑪ FOOT (FRONT)

I REQ'D

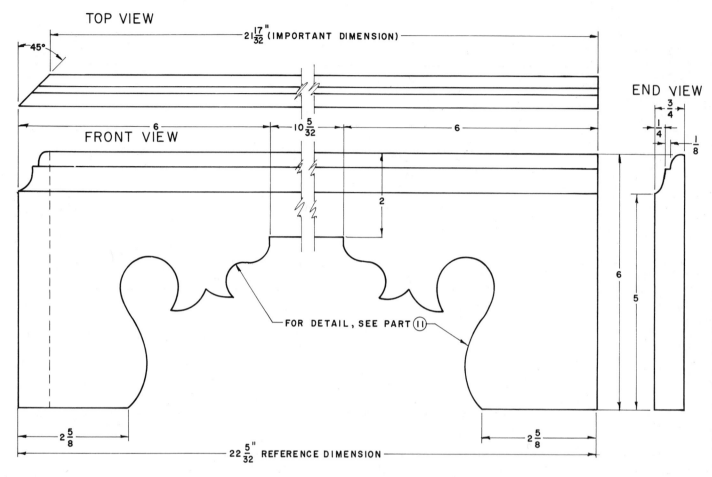

TOP VIEW

45°

$21\frac{17}{32}$" (IMPORTANT DIMENSION)

END VIEW

$\frac{3}{4}$

$\frac{1}{4}$

$\frac{1}{8}$

FRONT VIEW

6    $10\frac{5}{32}$ 6

2

6

5

FOR DETAIL, SEE PART ⑪

$2\frac{5}{8}$ $2\frac{5}{8}$

$22\frac{5}{32}$" REFERENCE DIMENSION

⑫ FOOT (SIDE)
I REQ'D AS SHOWN
I REQ'D OPPOSITE SHOWN

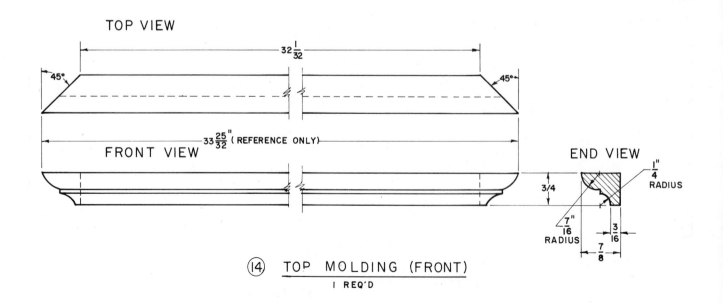

TOP VIEW

45° $32\frac{1}{32}$ 45°

$33\frac{25}{32}$" (REFERENCE ONLY)

FRONT VIEW

END VIEW

$\frac{1}{4}$" RADIUS

$\frac{3}{4}$

$\frac{7}{16}$" RADIUS

$\frac{3}{16}$

$\frac{7}{8}$

⑭ TOP MOLDING (FRONT)
I REQ'D

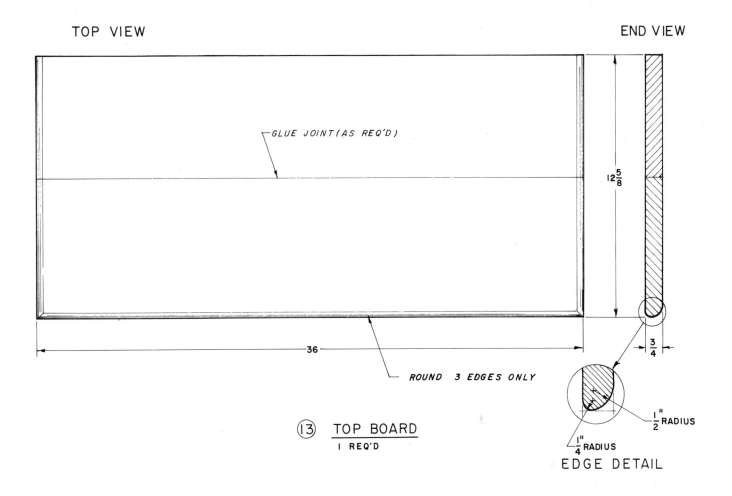

TOP VIEW

END VIEW

GLUE JOINT (AS REQ'D)

$12\frac{5}{8}$

36

ROUND 3 EDGES ONLY

⑬ TOP BOARD
1 REQ'D

$\frac{3}{4}$

$\frac{1}{2}$" RADIUS

$\frac{1}{4}$" RADIUS

EDGE DETAIL

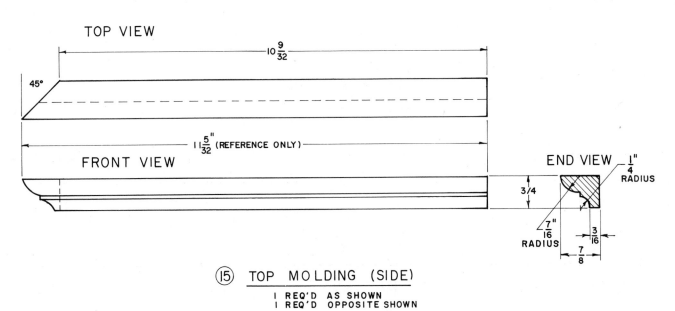

TOP VIEW

$10\frac{9}{32}$

45°

$11\frac{5}{32}$" (REFERENCE ONLY)

FRONT VIEW

END VIEW

$\frac{1}{4}$" RADIUS

3/4

$\frac{7}{16}$" RADIUS

$\frac{3}{16}$

$\frac{7}{8}$

⑮ TOP MOLDING (SIDE)
1 REQ'D AS SHOWN
1 REQ'D OPPOSITE SHOWN

FRONT VIEW

END VIEW

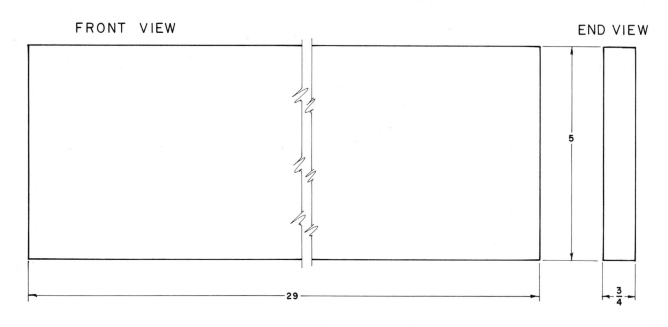

5

29

3/4

⑯ FRONT PANEL
2 REQ'D

FRONT VIEW

END VIEW

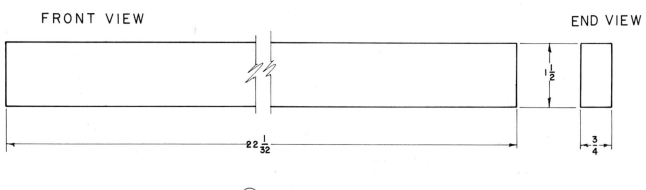

$1\frac{1}{2}$

$22\frac{1}{32}$

3/4

⑰ TOP SPACER
1 REQ'D

FRONT VIEW

END VIEW

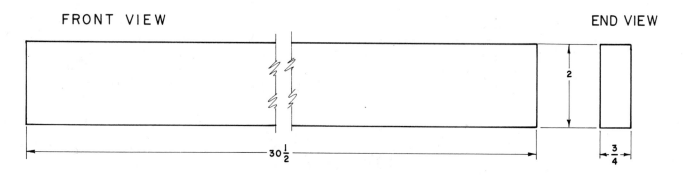

2

$30\frac{1}{2}$

3/4

⑱ DOOR STOP (TOP)
1 REQ'D

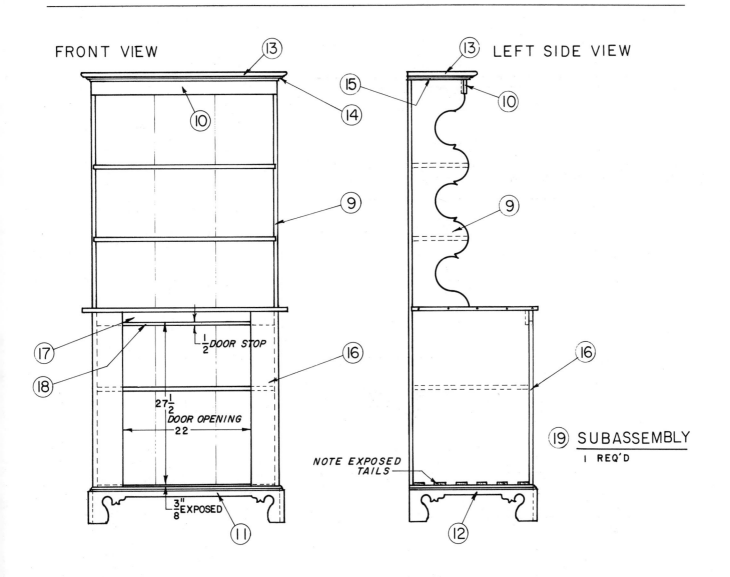

FRONT VIEW

⑬ ⑩ ⑭ ⑨ ⑰ ⑱ ½ DOOR STOP ⑯ 27½ DOOR OPENING 22 ⅜″ EXPOSED ⑪

LEFT SIDE VIEW

⑬ ⑮ ⑩ ⑨ ⑯ NOTE EXPOSED TAILS ⑫

⑲ SUBASSEMBLY
1 REQ'D

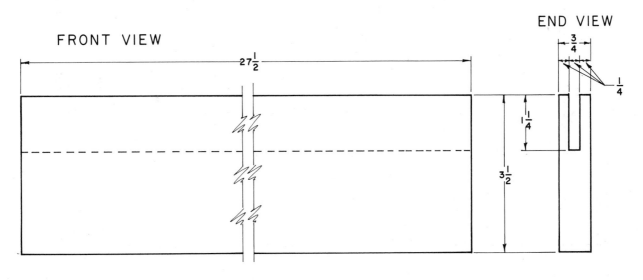

FRONT VIEW

27½

END VIEW

¾ ¼ 1¼ 3½

⑳ DOOR SIDE STILES
2 REQ'D

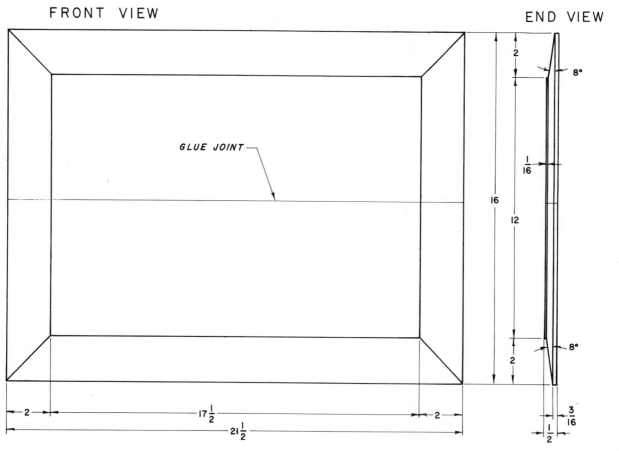

TONGUE
TOP VIEW
GROOVE
TONGUE

END VIEW

$17\frac{1}{2}$ REFERENCE DIMENSION

$1\frac{1}{4}$

15" (IMPORTANT DIMENSION)

$1\frac{1}{4}$

FRONT VIEW

GROOVE

$\frac{3}{4}$

$\frac{1}{4}$

GROOVE

$1\frac{1}{4}$

$3\frac{1}{2}$

TONGUE

TONGUE

㉑ DOOR TOP/BOTTOM RAIL
2 REQ'D

FRONT VIEW

END VIEW

GLUE JOINT

2

8°

$\frac{1}{16}$

16

12

8°

2

2

$17\frac{1}{2}$

2

$21\frac{1}{2}$

$\frac{3}{16}$

$\frac{1}{2}$

㉒ DOOR PANEL
1 REQ'D

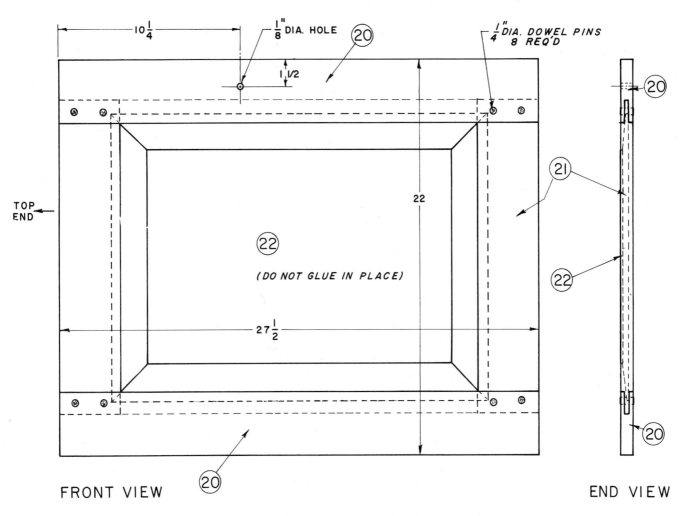

10¼

⅛" DIA. HOLE

20

¼" DIA. DOWEL PINS
8 REQ'D

1 1/2

20

21

22

TOP
END

22

(DO NOT GLUE IN PLACE)

27½

20

20

FRONT VIEW

END VIEW

23 DOOR SUBASSEMBLY
1 REQ'D

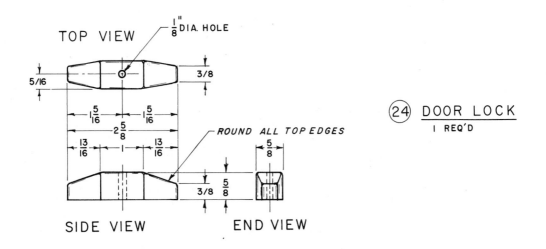

TOP VIEW

⅛" DIA. HOLE

5/16

3/8

1 5/16

1 5/16

2 5/8

13/16

13/16

ROUND ALL TOP EDGES

5/8

SIDE VIEW

3/8

5/8

END VIEW

24 DOOR LOCK
1 REQ'D

FRONT VIEW

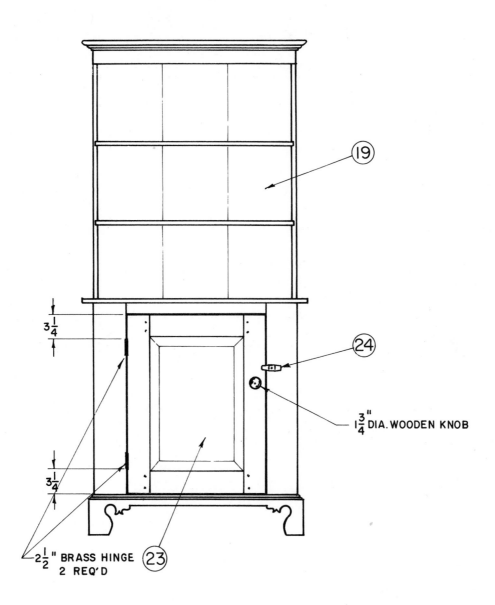

19

24

$1\frac{3}{4}$" DIA. WOODEN KNOB

$3\frac{1}{4}$

$3\frac{1}{4}$

$2\frac{1}{2}$" BRASS HINGE
2 REQ'D

23

25   ASSEMBLY

Suppliers

To make any antique project complete, the correct style, accessories, fasteners, stain, and paint must be used. Some of the many suppliers that can furnish you with items you need to complete your new "antique" furniture are listed below. This list is not complete, but should get you started. Many of these companies provide free catalogs of their products; others charge a nominal fee. Prices of their products vary also, so it does pay to compare both product and price. Clock supply companies offer top quality brass latches, hinges, and miscellaneous hardware, so a list of them has been included.

The listed woodworking-related magazines provide many tips and ideas for woodworking. Many send sample copies of their magazines for review by prospective subscribers.

CATALOG FOR MANY PRODUCTS

International Home Library
14439 North 73rd St.
Scottsdale, Arizona 85260

OLD-FASHIONED NAILS

Tremont Nail Co.
21 Elm St.
P.O. Box 111
Wareham, Massachusetts 02571

Horton Brasses
P.O. Box 95
Nooks Hill Rd.
Cromwell, Connecticut 06416

BRASS SCREWS

The Tool Works
76 9th Ave.
New York, New York 10011

Equality Screw Company, Inc.
P.O. Box 1296
El Cajon, California 92022

GENERAL CATALOGS

Constantine's
2065-C Eastchester Rd.
Bronx, New York 10461

Woodcraft Supply Corp.
313 Monvale Ave.
Woburn, Massachusetts 01888

John Harra Wood & Supply
39 West 19th St.
New York, New York 10011

Craftsman Wood Service Co.
1735 West Cortland Ct.
Addison, Illinois 60101

The Woodworkers Store
21801 Industrial Blvd.
Rogers, Minnesota 55374

Chaselle Arts and Crafts Inc.
9645 Gerwing Ln.
Columbia, Maryland 21046

Sax Arts and Crafts
P.O. Box 2002
Milwaukee, Wisconsin 53201

Nasco Arts and Crafts
901 Janesville Ave.
Atkinson, Wisconsin 53538

Industrial Arts Supply Co.
5724 West 36th St.
Minneapolis, Minnesota 55416

Pyramid Artists Material
Box 27
Urbana, Illinois 61801

FURNITURE HARDWARE

The Woodworkers Store
21810 Industrial Blvd.
Rogers, Minnesota 55374

Horton Brasses
P.O. Box 95
Nooks Hill Rd.
Cromwell, Connecticut 06416

Ritter & Son Hardware
Dept. WJ
Gualala, California 95445

Charolette Ford Trunks
Box 536
Spearman, Texas 74081

Paxton
Upper Falls, Maryland 21156

The Old Country Store
West Mansfield Village,
Massachusetts 02083

Old Guilford Forge
1840 Boston Post Rd.
Guilford, Connecticut 06437

Tech-Ni-Craft
Box 217
Auburn, Massachusetts 01501

Tremont Nail Co.
21 Elm St.
P.O. Box 111
Wareham, Massachusetts 02571

The Wise Co.
6503 St. Claude Ave.
Arabi, Louisiana 70032

Heirloom Antique Brass Co.
P.O. Box 146
Dundass, Minnesota 55019

The Decorative Hardware Studio
160 King St.
Chappaqua, New York 10514

Samuel Cabot Inc.
One Union St.
Boston, Massachusetts 02108

FINISHING PRODUCTS

The Knight Corp.
Box 894
Memphis, Tennessee 38101

Refinishing Products, Inc.
P.O. Box 788
Olive Branch, Mississippi 38654

Watco-Dennis Corp.
Michigan Ave. and 22nd St.
Santa Monica, California 90404

Deft Inc.
Dept F.
17451 Von Karman Ave.
Irvine, California 92714

General Finishers
P.O. Box 14363-F
Milwaukee, Wisconsin 53214

Cohassett Colonials
Cohassett, Massachusetts 02025

MILK PAINT

The Old-Fashioned Milk Paint Co.
Main St.
Groton, Massachusetts 01450

VENEERING

Bob Morgan Woodworking Supplies
1123 Bardstown Rd.
Louisville, Kentucky 40204

SPECIAL WOOD STOCK

Educational Lumber Co.
P.O. Box 5373
Asheville, North Carolina 28813

The Woodworkers Store
21801 Industrial Blvd.
Rogers, Minnesota 55374

Unicorn Universal Woods Ltd.
137 John St.
Toronto, Ontario M5V-2E4 Canada

Constantine's
2065-C Eastchester Rd.
Bronx, New York 10461

Maurice L. Condon Co., Inc.
248 Ferris Ave.
White Plains, New York 10603

The Sawmill
P.O. Box 329
Nazareth, Pennsylvania 18064

Wood World
9006 Waukegan Rd.
Morton Grove, Illinois 60053

Austin Hardwoods
2119 Goodrich
Austin, Texas 78701

Beauty-Wood Industries
91 Eglington Ave. E.
Mississauga, Ontario, Canada

CLOCK SUPPLIES

S. LaRose Inc.
234 Commerce Pl.
Greensboro, North Carolina 27420

H. DeCounick & Son
P.O. Box 68
200 Market Plaza
Alamo, California 94507

Mason & Sullivan Co.
Dept. 2112
Osterville, Massachusetts 02655

Emperor Clock Co.
Dept. 435
Emperor Industrial Park
Fairhope, Alabama 36532

Craft Products Co.
Dept. 14
2200 Dean St.
St. Charles, Illinois 60174

Merritt's Antiques Inc.
RD2
Douglassville, Pennsylvania 19518

Empire Clock Co.
1295 Rice St.
St. Paul, Minnesota 55117

Klockit
P.O. Box 629
Lake Geneva, Wisconsin 53147

WOODWORKING TOOLS

Brookstone Co.
Vose Farm Rd.
Peterborough, New Hampshire 03458

Silvo Hardware Co.
2205 Richmond St.
Philadelphia, Pennsylvania 19125

Woodcraft Supply Co.
313 Montvale Ave.
Woburn, Massachusetts 01888

The Woodworkers Store
21801 Industrial Blvd.
Rogers, Minnesota 55374

Greenlee Tool Division
2330 23rd Ave.
Rockford, Illinois 61101

The Toolroom
East Oxbow Rd. (780 FW)
Shelburne Falls, Massachusetts 01370

Constantine's
2065-C Eastchester Rd.
Bronx, New York 10461

Shopsmith Inc.
750 Center Drive
Vandalia, Ohio 45377

Armor Products
P.O. Box 290
Deer Park, New York 11729

Ball and Ball
463 W. Lincoln Highway
Exton, Pennsylvania 19341

Frog Tool Co. Ltd.
700 W. Jackson Blvd.
Dept. 5E
Chicago, Illinois 60606

Woodworker's Supply
of New Mexico
5604 Alameda, N.E.
Albuquerque, New Mexico 87113

Conover Woodcraft Specialties
18124 Madison Rd.
Parkman, Ohio 44080

U.S. General Supply Corp.
Dept. A-309
100 General Pl.
Jericho, New York 11753

The Fine Tool Shops
P.O. Box 1262
20 Backus Ave.
Danbury, Connecticut 06810

RELATED PUBLICATIONS (MAGAZINES)

Fine Woodworking
The Taunton Press
52 Church Hill Rd.
Box 355
Newton, Connecticut 06470

The Woodworker's Journal
Dept. SL
Box 1629
New Milford, Connecticut 06776

Workbench Magazine
Box 5965
Kansas City, Missouri 64111

Index